Wind Toys

That Spin, Sing, Twirl & Whirl

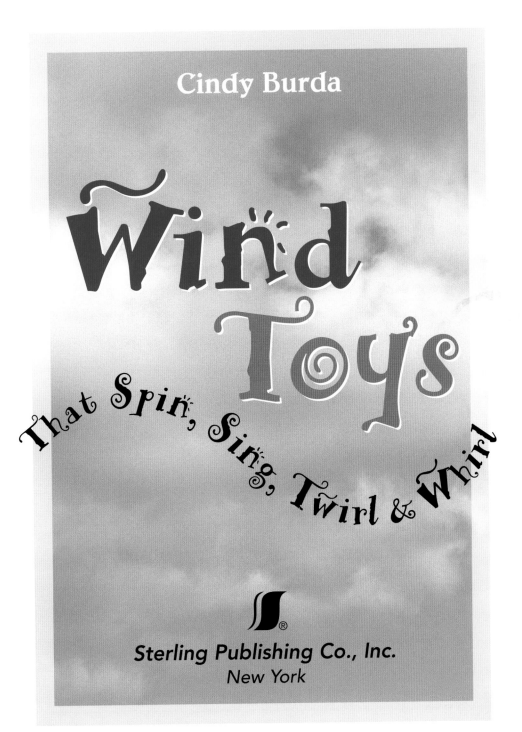

Cindy Burda

Wind Toys

That Spin, Sing, Twirl & Whirl

Sterling Publishing Co., Inc.
New York

Editor: Chris Rich
Art and production: Thom Gaines
Photography: Evan Bracken
Illustrations: Bernadette Wolf
Assistant editor: Catharine Sutherland
Editorial assistance: Heather Smith

Library of Congress Cataloging-in-Publication Data
Burda, Cindy, 1972-
    Wind Toys that Spin, Sing, Whirl & Twirl / by Cindy Burda
       p.   Cm.
    Includes indexes.
    ISBN 0-8069-3934-6
    1. Handicraft. 2. Whirligigs. 3. Wind chimes. 4. Banners
    5. Weather vanes.   I. Title.
    TT157.B82   1999
    745.5—dc21   98-47127
                                        CIP

1 3 5 7 9 10 8 6 4 2

Published by Sterling Publishing Company, Inc.
387 Park Avenue South
New York, N.Y. 10016

Created and produced by Altamont Press, Inc.
50 College Street, Asheville, NC 28801

© 1999 by Sterling Publishing Company, Inc.

Distributed in Canada by Sterling Publishing
    c/o Canadian Manda Group, One Atlantic Avenue, Suite 105
    Toronto, Ontario, Canada M6K 3E7
Distributed in Great Britain and Europe by Chris Lloyd
    463 Ashley Road, Parkstone, Poole, Dorset, BH14 0AX, United Kingdom
Distributed in Australia by Capricorn Link (Australia) Pty Ltd.
    P.O. Box 6651, Baulkham Hills, Business Centre, NSW 2153, Australia

Sterling ISBN 0-8069-3934-6

Table of Contents

Introduction

Mother Nature gave us a wonderful gift when she set the first winds into motion. Think of all the ways in which we've put that gift to use. As long ago as A.D. 500, the Persians were pumping water and grinding grain with windmills. In the fourteenth century, explorers and adventurers traversed the globe in ships powered by strong ocean winds; in their travels, they discovered a whole New World. A few centuries later, water-pumping windmills turned that New World's vast western deserts into bountiful farm land. Today, thousands of gleaming, modern wind turbines spin out clean, inexpensive electricity that runs everything from home computers to city street lights. The wind has truly been a driving force in history.

But think for a moment of all the other ways in which we simply enjoy the wind. Remember your delight the first time you saw a tiny puff of breeze turn a bunch of fallen leaves into a whirlwind of color and motion? And is there anything that can make you feel cozier than the wind blowing and howling outside while you sit tucked in bed with a big cup of hot chocolate? Well, this book features more than 35 creative, new ways for you to celebrate and enjoy this wonderful natural resource—from flowing banners and fanciful windsocks to spinning whirligigs and singing chimes. With such a wide variety to choose from,

crafters in every field and of every skill level are sure to find projects to try.

Woodworkers will delight in making clever whirligigs and wooden wind vanes. The When-Pigs-Fly wind vane on page 52 is the perfect starting point for beginners, while the ingenious Centipede whirligig on page 101 will inspire experts. Folks with a fondness for fabrics will enjoy creating gorgeous windsocks and stunning sewn, painted, and dyed banners. Even clay lovers and metalsmiths will find a project or two to their taste.

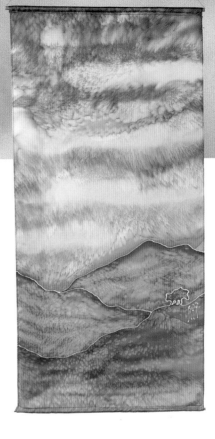

Don't worry if you see something you like that requires a technique you've never tried before. The detailed instructions with each project will guide you through every step. If you're a little timid about trying something totally new, turn to Chapter 1; although it's not a comprehensive beginner's course for crafters, it will give you an introduction to every major technique used in the book. If your timidity remains, and you're still not totally confident about picking up a jigsaw or sitting down at a sewing machine for the first time, you'll find dozens of books in your local library to fill in any gaps.

If you're like most crafters, you probably don't have a sophisticated workshop full of specialized equipment. Not to worry! As you browse through the book, you'll notice that very few of the projects require special tools or materials. You probably have many of the tools you'll need right in your sewing basket or hanging over your work bench. Those that you don't have can be easily found at your local hardware and art- and craft-supply stores. If you're not sure where to look for a material or tool, chances are that the "Tips" that proceed many of the projects will point you in the right direction.

You'll notice that the projects in this book are unique. A really talented group of crafters and artists submitted the work and instructions featured in the following pages. Their ingenuity will give you hours of fun as you browse, choosing which project to try first. Follow the clear and detailed instructions to recreate their projects, or use their ingenuity as a springboard for experimenting with completely new designs.

You'll soon see how easy wind toys are to personalize and make all your own. Let your neighbors down the street decorate their homes with mass-manufactured, prefabricated banners. Your banner will be a one-of-a-kind, original design. Leave the store-bought wind chimes to the neighbors, too. With the instructions on pages 12-13, you'll easily be able to craft custom-tuned wind chimes, made to sing at any pitch you like.

So what are you waiting for? The next good breeze is just around the bend. Be ready to greet it in proper style.

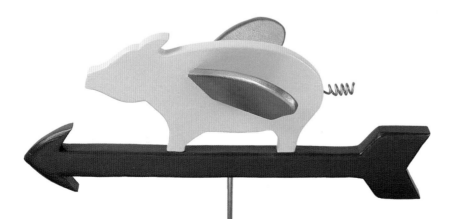

Chapter 1

Learning the Basics

The projects that begin on page 22 range from dyed and painted banners to simple wind vanes and intricate wooden whirligigs. Don't be daunted by the ones that seem complex. Even if you've never touched a sewing machine or coping saw before, many of these fascinating wind toys are well within reach of beginners. You don't have to be a woodworking pro to make an amusing wind vane, an expert seamstress to complete a stunning banner, or a stained-glass artisan to make a colorful glass wind chime.

Start by browsing through the project pages. Choose a project that appeals to you and read the instructions that come with it. If the required tools and techniques aren't familiar to you, return to this chapter, where you'll find brief descriptions of a wide range of techniques, from dyeing and painting fabrics to working with metal, glass, and wood.

Although these pages don't offer a complete introductory course in any of the techniques, they do provide invaluable explanations and tips—information that will help you enjoy making a wind toy as much as you enjoy the final product. If you're still puzzled by a tool or technique, enlist the help of a friend who has some experience making the type of project you've selected, or check out a good book from your local library. Never hesitate to ask the experts, either. Most crafters enjoy sharing their skills with people who are truly eager to learn them!

Working with Fabric

Textile lovers will find a passel of exciting fabric projects in this book. Following is a brief review of the basic techniques required to make them.

Sewing

If you have a sewing machine, you're well on your way. A couple of projects call for a satin-stitch or open-toe embroidery foot, and if you have a gridded cutting mat and rotary cutter, naturally, these are very useful, too. Otherwise, a tape measure and good scissors will serve you well.

None of the sewn projects in this book requires difficult or unfamiliar techniques, and even beginning sewers will find at least one or two banners or windsocks to try. Perhaps the only new experience will be working with rip-

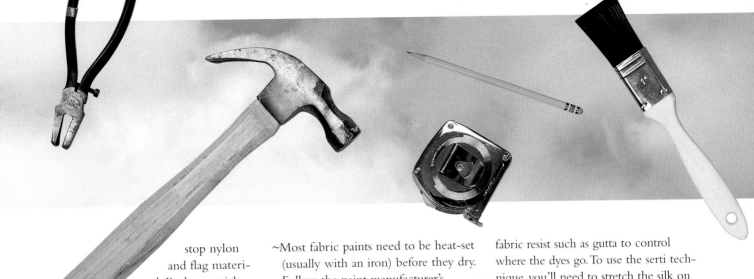

stop nylon and flag material. Both materials are great for making projects that will be subjected to sun, wind, and rain, and most fabric stores carry or can order them.

The one difficulty you may encounter with ripstop nylon is fraying. The best ways to avoid this are to cut the fabric with pinking shears or an electric hot knife, or to cut along the fabric's diagonal with regular scissors or a rotary cutter. Even when the project instructions don't call for it, you may want to take a few minutes and a few stitches to hem cut edges—doing so will add many windy days to your project's life.

Painting Fabrics

What is a painter's canvas but a big swatch of cloth? And what better way to make an artistic statement than by turning that swatch into a personalized banner, ready to be flown from the nearest flagpole? The following tricks and tips for painting fabrics will speed your progress and improve the finished product.

~Wash and iron the fabric before you do anything else.

~Textile or fabric paints, made especially for use on fabric, are your best bet. Read the paint manufacturer's instructions and recommendations. Then read them again!

~Most fabric paints need to be heat-set (usually with an iron) before they dry. Follow the paint manufacturer's instructions for heat-setting.

~Paint tends to bleed through fabrics, so be sure to protect your work surface with several layers of newspaper.

~If you're more comfortable filling in the colors of a pre-drawn design, and you're working with a relatively sheer fabric, simply start by drawing your design on plain white paper with a black felt-tip pen. Place the design under the fabric and follow it while you paint. You can also transfer the design directly to the fabric with tracing paper. Trace the design onto the tracing paper, turn the paper to the back side, and trace over the lines with a transfer pencil (carried by most craft and fabric stores). Place the design on the fabric, transfer side down, and press with a warm iron.

~On a stylistic note, you'll find that broad areas of color look best when accented with fine lines of darker colors. You'll want to use this technique in particular for the Flower Garden banners on pages 76-77.

Dyeing Fabrics

You'll find three techniques for dyeing fabrics in this book: serti, marbling, and batik.

Serti (or Fencing)

Serti, or fencing, is a method of painting on silk with fiber-reactive dyes, using a fabric resist such as gutta to control where the dyes go. To use the serti technique, you'll need to stretch the silk on a frame. An old picture frame is perfect for small pieces of silk, but if you don't have one, you can easily build a frame.

To make a frame approximately 4' x 4', cut two 8' pine 1 x 2s into four equal pieces with a circular or crosscut saw. Lay the boards out in a square and fasten them at each corner with two No. 6 x 1½" wood screws. The project instructions on page 88 will tell you exactly how to stretch the silk in the frame.

You'll also need a paintbrush for each color of dye you use and a plastic applicator bottle with a fine tip and metal tip attachment to apply the resist.

Marbling

With marbling, you apply fabric paints to the surface of a specially prepared bath and swirl the paints into patterns; then you place a piece of treated fabric on top of the paints to pick up the patterns. Technically, when you marble you're really painting—not dyeing—because, while paints merely adhere to the fabric's surface, dyes actually penetrate the fabric and chemically bond with it. Nevertheless, the process of marbling is much more like dyeing than painting, so that's why it's included in this section.

To marble, you'll need a tub to hold the bath. The tub should be large enough to hold your piece of fabric stretched flat. You'll also need plastic applicator bottles, one for each color of paint you use; and tools to sprinkle, spread, and shape the paints on the bath—whisks, hair picks, and chopsticks all work well. And, of course, you should always protect your hands with a pair of rubber gloves.

Batik

With batik, you dye patterns into fabric by covering and protecting some areas of the material with wax.

As with the serti technique, the fabric is stretched in a frame; the same kind of frame works just as well for batik as for serti. You'll also need a small electric deep-fat fryer or a thermostatically-controlled heavy metal pot or pan for melting wax. Whatever appliance you use, be sure that it has an accurate temperature gauge. You'll

apply the molten wax to the fabric with stiff-bristled paintbrushes and a "tjanting." A tjanting consists of a small, spouted metal cup on the end of a heat-resistant wooden handle. It allows precise placement of lines and dots of wax and is essential for detailed designs. Most good art- and craft-supply stores sell these special tools in a variety of sizes. You'll also need a large tub for the dye baths, and rubber gloves to keep your hands safe.

Although batik isn't at all difficult, some of the steps require a little more information than is given in the project instructions on pages 85-86. Following is a quick run through of the batik process.

Start by washing, drying, and ironing the fabric to be batiked. Either draw the design you want right on the fabric or transfer it by following the

directions given on page 9 with the painting tips. Then stretch the fabric in a frame. Prepare the first dye bath according to the dye manufacturer's directions. Use only cold water fiber-reactive dyes for batik—never paints or other kinds of dyes.

Warm beeswax or commercial batik wax in an electric deep-fat fryer or a thermostatically-controlled pot or pan. Heat the wax slowly until it flows like water and easily penetrates the fabric to be dyed. In general, you'll want the wax to be about 270°F. Most kinds of wax have flash points of between 400°F and 500°F; you should avoid letting your wax get that hot. (The flash point is the lowest temperature at which the vapors from the melted wax can ignite in the air.)

Apply the molten wax to the stretched fabric with paintbrushes and a tjanting. (Use the paintbrushes to cover larger areas, and the tjanting for detail work.) Make sure the wax penetrates the fabric completely. Let the wax dry; then start dyeing the fabric. The project instructions on page 86 will guide you through the dyeing steps.

When the batik is complete, you must remove the wax, a process that must be performed outdoors or in a well-ventilated area. Sandwich the fabric between sheets of plain newsprint and apply an iron, using the cotton setting. Remove the waxy newsprint and replace it with fresh sheets until you've lifted all the heavy wax from the fabric. Have the final project professionally dry-cleaned.

Working with Metal

Most of the metalwork projects in this book are easy to make with simple tools; a couple involve more complex techniques.

metal parts together. Brazing, which is similar to soldering, is the process of joining metal pieces by melting a thin rod of metal alloy (a brazing rod) into the joint. You should always select brazing rods that will melt at lower temperatures than the metal pieces you wish to braze together.

If you've never cut metal or brazed with a torch before, first browse through the information that follows. Then, if you'd like to enter the world of metalsmithing, register for a good basic welding class or ask a professional for some lessons. Working successfully and safely with a torch—a tremendously exciting process—involves much more information than this book can provide.

At the top of the photo below, you'll see an oxy-acetylene torch. Two supply hoses connect to its base and deliver oxygen and acetylene, which are stored

Simple Metalwork

You'll use a hacksaw to cut metal tubes and rods, a file to smooth rough metal edges, tin snips to cut shapes from metal sheets, and a chisel and hammer or mallet to make cutouts in thin metal.

Hacksaws, which are made specifically to cut metal, look a bit like coping saws (see page 15), but their blades are about ½"-wide. One tip: These saws cut only on the forward stroke, as you push the saw away from you.

Tin snips look a bit like garden shears, but their powerful blades cut through thin metal sheets with ease. Chisels, with their sharp blade tips, will dent or cut through metal when their handles are struck with a mallet.

Cutting and Brazing with a Torch

The cut and brazed projects on pages 54-58 require some expertise with a more complex tool—an oxy-acetylene torch. This torch is used to cut through thick sheets of metal and to "braze"

in separate tanks. The torch has two regulators—one for oxygen and the other for acetylene—that allow you to control the flame by controlling the mixture that feeds it; different flames are required for different jobs. Attached to the top of the torch is an exchangeable "head" from which the flame emerges. Heads come in different shapes and sizes, each designed for a specific task.

Also shown in this photo are a number of important tools and accessories used in conjunction with the torch. Safety equipment is a must. You'll need two sets of goggles: a clear set to protect your eyes as you clean the metal; and a pair of #5 welder's goggles, the dark lenses of which protect your eyes from the brightness of the flame. A respirator is also necessary, as the fumes created during brazing and cutting can be dangerous to inhale. Welder's gloves or very thick leather gloves will help prevent burns, as will clothing that covers as much of your body as possible.

To make the brazed projects in this book, you'll also need a work surface (a ⅜"-thick plate steel surface is ideal, but you can also work on top of concrete); a wire brush or grinder for cleaning metal; welder's chalk for marking pattern outlines on the metal that you plan to cut with your torch; pliers for holding hot metal; brazing rods; and flux powder, into which you'll dip the rods before heating them.

Brazing is a multistep process that begins with cleaning the metal pieces; a grinding wheel or wire brush works well. You'll also use the grinding wheel or a chisel to remove any "slag" (metal deposits left from cutting the metal with a torch). You'll then position the clean metal parts next to each other and clamp them in place. After heating the metal surrounding the joint, you'll dip the end of your brazing rod into flux and then melt the brazing rod into the joint.

Making Metal Wind-Chime Tubes

Commercial wind-chime tubes are simply pieces of hollow metal tubing. They're sometimes available from craft stores and can always be recycled from manufactured chimes. Making your own, however, is easy. Just purchase rigid metal tubing at a hardware or plumbing-supply store and cut sections from it with a hacksaw. To suspend the tubes, drill a pair of holes through each one and run cord or monofilament though the holes. A drill press is the ideal tool for drilling the holes, but if you don't own one, use an electric drill and a ¹⁄₁₆" split-point bit. Clamp the tube securely on top of some scrap wood before you start, and use a hammer and nail to make a dent at the future hole location. (The dent will prevent your drill bit from slipping out of place.)

Tuning Metal Chimes

Any material can be used to make chimes, as long as the chimes will "sing" when they strike each other or another object. If you care about *what* the chimes sing, however, you'll definitely want to make the project on pages 22-23. Eric Reiswig, who designed this musical chime, tuned the tubes to a minor pentatonic scale by drilling their hanger holes at specific locations.

If you're a musician at heart and/or by training, you can go one step farther and create wind-chime tubes that are not only tuned to each other but that are also tuned to a specific pitch—chimes, in other words, that will play middle C, middle G, etc. Why would you want to do this? Imagine sitting on your porch, listening to two sets of chimes that actually "sing" in harmony! Here's how to bring that fantasy to life:

First, you'll need a piano or an electric tuner. You'll also need a good music text that provides the frequencies of notes. Next, buy some metal tubing. Any metal will do, as long as the tubes you cut from it are made of the same metal and are of the same thickness and diameter. Your goal is to create tubes that sound at the same pitch. Different metals and different thicknesses of the same metal will sound at different pitches, so don't mix and match tubes with different densities, thicknesses, or diameters.

Start by reading through the project instructions on pages 22-23; they'll give you some idea of basic tuning procedures for wind chimes. Next, cut a relatively long chime from the metal tubing to serve as a "reference tube." (You'll shorten this tube as you work.) Measure and record the tube's length. Then calculate 22.5% of that length. Measuring from either end of the tube, mark the 22.5% length on the tube. Attach a rubber band or cord around the tube at that mark and hang the tube up.

Using a hacksaw, shorten the tube, little by little, until it plays a specific note when struck by another length of the tubing. Remember that each time you shorten the tube, you must reposition the rubber band or cord at 22.5% of the tube's length. When the tube plays the desired note, measure its length, write that down, and label it "L1." Now, in your music book, find the frequency of the note that your reference tube plays. Record this frequency and label it "F1."

Look up the frequency of the note that you'd like the next wind-chime tube to play. If your reference tube, for example, plays middle C, and you'd like the next tube to play middle G, look up the frequency of middle G, write it down and label it "F2." To find out how long to make this new tube (or "L2"), use the following formula:

$$L_2 = L_1 \sqrt{\frac{F_1}{F_2}}$$

F_1 is the frequency of the reference tube.

L_1 is the reference tube's length.

F_2 is the frequency of the note desired for the new tube.

L_2 is the required length of the new tube.

Repeat these steps to cut as many tubes as you like. Then determine where to place the hanger holes (a critical step) by calculating 22.5% of each tube's length. Measure and mark that distance from either end of the tube and drill the pair of hanger holes at the mark.

Working with Wood

Before you read this entire section, keep a couple of things in mind. First, you won't need every tool that's described in it, even if you build every whirligig and wind vane in this book! Many of the tools are ones that experienced woodworkers use and that you may want to purchase at some point; however, weekend hobbyists can almost always substitute less expensive and simpler tools. A handheld coping saw, for example, can do much of the work that a scroll saw or band saw can do; it just does the work a bit slower. Second, you don't need to plow through this section word by word. Instead, choose a project, take a look at the "Tools" list and instructions that come with it, and if you need to know more about the required tools and techniques, look them up here. In other words: Relax! Even a beginner can build most of these woodworking projects with a few basic hand tools.

Selecting Wood

Most of the wood that's required for these projects falls into one of four categories: commercial softwood (see the chart on page 126); exterior-grade plywood; craft wood; and round wooden dowels. You'll find softwood, plywood, and dowels at your local building-supply store; and thin plywood and craft wood at a craft or hobby shop.

In a few instances, the project designers used hardwoods of specific thicknesses. These aren't usually available commercially. If you don't own the stationary power tools required to produce lumber of specific thicknesses, you can easily substitute standard softwoods by adapting the project measurements.

When you purchase wood for these projects, try to handpick your lumber, checking each piece for defects as you do. These defects include checks (or splits) in the wood, knotholes, wane (edges that are rounded) and warpage (bends or twists in the boards).

Tools and Techniques

Always check the lists provided with any woodworking project before you go out on a shopping spree. You'll save yourself a lot of time and money!

Workbench

Although no serious woodworking enthusiast would dream of doing without a high-quality workbench, many weekend hobbyists make do without. Any work surface that's solid, stable, and set at a comfortable height will do. A wobbling surface just won't work.

Clamping

Clamps, which come in different styles and sizes, are used to hold one or more pieces of wood in place as they're marked or drilled, or after they're glued. The type you're most likely to use in these projects are C-clamps (see the photo on the next page). At one end of the clamp's C-shaped steel frame is a threaded rod with a small pad. When the rod is turned, the pad

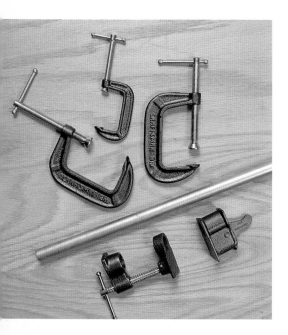

moves toward or away from the other (fixed) end of the frame. To clamp one or more pieces of wood, the wood is placed between the ends of the frame and the rod is turned until the pad holds the wood firmly against the fixed end of the clamp.

Also shown in the photo above are pipe clamps. Although you may not use them much while making these projects, they're great for larger jobs such as gluing a series of boards together edge-to-edge.

The "frame" of a pipe clamp is actually a long metal bar. The fixed end of the clamp is a fixture that's threaded onto one end of the bar; the movable portion of the clamp is a fixture that slides along the pipe and can be locked in any position.

Clamps of any kind can mar wood, so always insert rubber pads or thin pieces of wood between the wood you're clamping and the ends of the clamp.

A vise is just another version of a clamp, but it's usually mounted on a workbench. You'll find that this piece of equipment comes in handy when you need to drill holes in wind-chime tubes.

Measuring

Have you ever heard the old saying, "Measure twice, cut once"? Here's what it means: If you take the time to double-check every measurement before marking and cutting your wood, you'll only need to cut the wood once. Carelessly taken measurements almost always result in wasted wood and time.

A steel tape measure is one of those household tools you'll never be sorry you bought. The flexible metal tape, which is coiled inside a metal case, unwinds when you pull on its end, and on high-quality models can be locked so it won't wind itself back up. Get a 25'-long, ¾"- or 1"-wide tape (the narrower ones are flimsier). The first 12' of the tape should be marked in ¹⁄₁₆" increments.

A 12" or 24" straightedge (or steel ruler) will prove useful when you need to mark straight lines.

A combination square (shown in the photo below) has a handle that can be moved up and down the tool's ruler base. This handle can be locked in position at any point and can measure 45° and 90° angles. The tool is used to mark straight lines across boards, to measure lengths, and to mark points at specific distances from the edges of boards.

A sliding T-bevel, also shown in the photo below, is useful for marking or checking angles. Its blade pivots on the handle and can be locked in place at any angle.

A level is a useful addition to any do-it-yourselfer's tool collection and will help you set up wind vanes on their posts. A carpenter's square is most frequently used for large construction jobs, but can also take the place of a straightedge when you need to measure and mark straight lines.

A compass, with its two legs, is used to mark circles. One leg is pointed and the other holds a pencil.

A woodworking protractor, which consists of a flat semicircle of steel with an opening in the center, is used to

measure and mark angles. The 180°
scale is marked on both the inner and
outer edges of the steel blade. A pivot-
ing indicator on the tool can be adjusted to point to the correct angle.

Cutting and Drilling

Don't think for a minute that you'll
need every cutting tool described in
this section! A coping saw or its electric counterpart—a jigsaw—will do
most cutting jobs well.

The photo to the right includes a
crosscut saw, a coping saw, and a couple
of wood chisels. Crosscut saws are used
to cut wood across its grain, as you do
when you cut a short length from a
long board. Ripsaws are used to cut
along (or with) the grain, as you do
when you cut a board to make its wide
face thinner. In a pinch, you can rip
with a crosscut saw, but you can't use a
ripsaw to make a crosscut.

When you purchase saws, you'll
notice that blades comes with "points
per inch" information. This number
indicates how closely the teeth on the
saw's edge are to each other—the
more points per inch, the closer the
teeth, and the finer your cut will be.
Crosscut saws generally have 7 to 12
points per inch; ripsaws come with 4½
to 7 points per inch.

A coping saw, with its very thin,
replaceable blade, is great for cutting
curved shapes, especially if you don't
own a jigsaw. The coping saw is held
vertically as it cuts.

A set of standard, bevel-edged
woodworking chisels (known as cabi-
netmaker's chisels) will allow you to
pare and shave wood. A rubber mallet
is used to strike the chisel handles.

For scribing and cutting wood, nothing is quite as helpful as a utility knife.
On better models, the blade can be
retracted so you don't hurt yourself when
you're not using it, and the extra blades
can be stored safely in the knife casing.

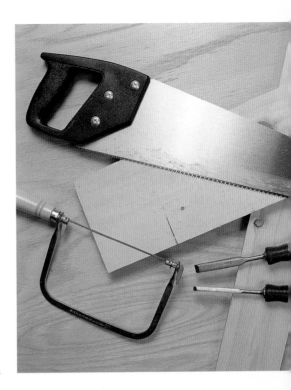

Some of the projects in this book
require carving small pieces of wood.
Any small carving knife with a sharp
blade and a handle that fits comfortably
into your palm will work.

The photo below shows a circular
saw and a jigsaw. The circular saw, with
its "combination" blade, is the power-
driven version of crosscut saws and ripsaws. The round blade can be adjusted
to cut at 90° and 45° angles or at any
angle between. When it's set to cut at
an ordinary 90° angle, the blade bites
down into the wood up to 2¼"; this
bite decreases a bit when the blade is
tilted to cut at an angle.

For cutting curved shapes and interior holes, a jigsaw takes the place of a
coping saw. (A coping saw will usually
work, but an electric jigsaw is much
more versatile.) The "bayonet" blade on

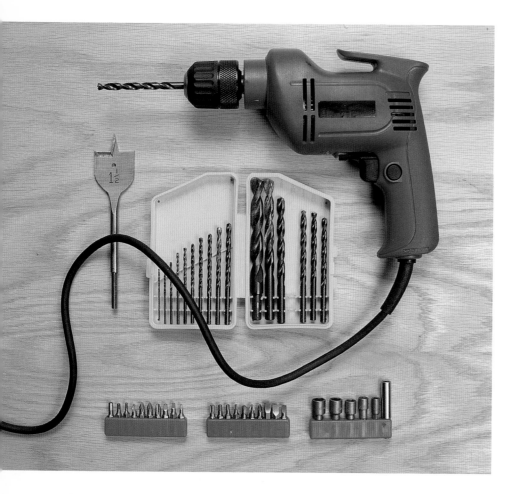

sandpaper surface or an aluminum oxide surface will work well on wood.

For many of the woodworking projects, you'll need a ⅜" variable-speed power drill (or a hand drill) with a full set of bits (they needn't be expensive). Cordless drills are fine for weekend work, but if you'd like to use your drill for home-improvement or other construction tasks, stick with a model that has an electric cord.

If you've never used a power drill before, following is a description of how it works. The barrel of this tool has a chuck at its open end. You fit the drill bit into the chuck and twist the chuck to tighten it around the bit. When you squeeze the trigger, the bit turns, boring a hole in your wood or metal. You control the speed of the turning bit by the varying the amount of pressure you exert on the trigger. Most power drills come with a reversible motor, too, which allows you to reverse the direction of the spinning bit—a very handy trick when you need to remove screws.

In some situations, you may need to drill a hole to a specific depth. Depth control collars—small metal rings that fit around the base of the drill bit—keep the bit from drilling too deep. A quick and easy alternative is to wrap a piece of masking tape around the bit to serve as a visual cue.

Different drill bits are made for different jobs. For these projects, brad-point bits will be the most useful. These bits have points that keep them from sliding across the wood when you first start to bore holes. You may want to add a set of countersink bits to your tool collection, as well. These cut shallow slopes at the top of each hole so that when you drive a wood screw into the countersunk hole, its head will rest flush with the wood instead of protruding above it. For a couple of the projects, you'll need

this tool moves rapidly up and down and the tool can cut at a 45° angle as well. If you purchase a jigsaw, get one with a variable speed control and an orbital blade action (the blade on these models moves forward and back as well as up and down).

Serious woodworkers often have stationary power saws in their workshops, including table saws, band saws, and scroll saws. There's no doubt that these tools make many cutting tasks much easier. A table saw is bit like a powerful circular saw that is built into a frame and table; the circular blade emerges from the table top. A scroll saw is much like a stationary jigsaw; the narrow blade emerges from the table and moves rapidly up and down. The band saw, another stationary power tool, has a blade that is a continuous

band of steel. This band cuts as it rotates within its fixed frame.

Rasps, wood files, and sanders are used to remove excess wood. Rasps make the coarsest "cuts" and sanders make the smoothest. In many of the woodworking projects in this book, you'll skip the rasping and filing stages and use only sandpaper.

A handheld sanding block—the kind that's operated with plenty of elbow-grease—will do a fine job for rough-sanding many wooden parts, but for intricately carved wooden pieces such as those in many whirligigs, you'll probably find it easier to hold the sand-paper in your hand. Sandpaper comes in different "grits," the coarsest being No. 60 and the finest being No. 220. Always start with a coarse grit and finish up with a fine one. Either a garnet spade bits or hole saws—two types of bits made for cutting holes. Among the many other bits available are screwdriver and wrench bits.

Fastening

For most simple woodworking projects, a No. 2 Phillips-head and a No. 2 flat-bladed screwdriver will come in handy. If you have an electric drill, you can use screwdriver bits instead. A 6- to 12-ounce claw hammer with a forged steel head will work well for driving large nails; a tack hammer will do a better job on small nails. A nail set, which looks a bit like a short metal pencil is useful for "sinking" nails below the surface of the wood in order to hide them. You place the narrow end of the nail set on top of the nail head and strike the wide end with your hammer.

Most wooden projects parts are fastened with glue and either nails or screws. For open-grained softwoods such as the ones you'll most likely use for these projects, any common, yellow woodworker's glue (aliphatic resin) will do. This glue dries slowly and ensures strong joints. You may want to try a quick-drying epoxy resin glue instead, but this glue is generally used with hardwoods. On wooden parts that you don't plan to paint or varnish, use a waterproof glue such as resorcinol resin—the glue used in boat building.

Most of the nails you'll use for your wind-driven projects will be finish nails and wire brads. The very small heads on these nails allow you to drive the nails below the wood surface. You may fill any holes above the nail heads with wood filler and sand the filler smooth.

Wood screws are common fasteners, and work especially well when they're used in conjunction with glue. A few of the projects in this book also call for drywall screws, which have coarser threads than wood screws.

You'd be amazed by how many ways there are to join and fasten two pieces of wood. Fortunately, you'll only be using a few standard joints for these projects: butt joints, lap joints, half-lap joints, and dowel joints. (The project instructions will walk you through every step.)

To make a butt joint, all you do is butt the end of one board up against the face of another. To make a lap joint, you fasten the wide face of one board to the wide face of another.

Half-lap joints are slightly more complex. Suppose you'd like to join two pieces of wood to make a cross-shaped hanger for a mobile (see the photo on page 25). Rather than attaching one piece on top of the other, you'd remove a notch from the face of each piece and then fit the notches together.

Here's a tip on cutting the notches for a half-lap joint with a coping saw: First, take a look at figure 3 on page 26, which shows the notches. To cut each notch, first mark two lines across the piece of wood. Clamp the wood securely and use a coping saw to cut a series of parallel cuts between the marks. Make the cuts as deep as you'd like the notch to be and as close to each other as possible. To remove the last bits of wood, clean out the notch with a sharp carving knife or chisel.

Dowel joints are made by using lengths of dowel as "pins" to hold two pieces of wood. You drill holes in the wooden parts first. Then you apply some glue inside the holes and insert the dowel. A rubber mallet works well for pounding the dowel into one hole and for forcing the hole in the other board over the dowel in the first board.

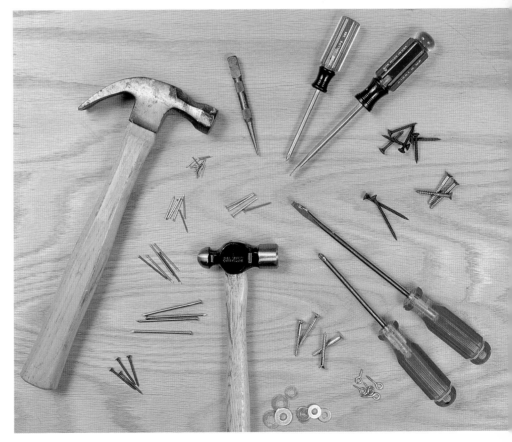

The only challenging part of making a dowel joint is aligning the two holes in two pieces of wood. To make the job easier, you may want to purchase a dowel jig—a piece of equipment that aligns the drill bit accurately.

Finishing

Wood that's exposed to the elements will eventually rot, and softwoods are especially vulnerable. To ensure a reasonable life span for your whirligigs, wind vanes, and wooden wind chimes, be sure to finish the wood with a protective coating such as exterior paint or—if you'd prefer a clear finish—polyurethane spar varnish. (Two coats work better than one.)

Working with Polymer Clay

Crafters have used this fun and versatile material to make everything from beads to birdhouses. Although polymer clay is very easy to use, you should know the basics before getting started.

Your hands are the most important tools of all for this craft. You'll also want a sharp, flat blade with a broad cutting surface; the one shown in the photo above is perfect. A tool with a sharp metal point will come in handy for shaping, and you'll need a rolling pin or pasta machine to flatten the clay into sheets. (Do keep in mind that after you've used kitchen utensils for polymer clay work, you should never use them for preparing food.) Plastic laminates and bristol boards make the best work surfaces; glass, acrylic, and porous materials should be avoided. You'll bake your polymer clay creations in an ordinary kitchen oven (not a microwave).

Each brand of polymer clay has unique characteristics, so start by reading the manufacturer's instructions and cautions. The next step is to "condition" the clay before you actually begin using it. The easiest method of conditioning is simply to start by warming a small amount of clay in your hands. Roll it into a ball; then roll the ball into a log. Stretch, twist, and fold the log back onto itself until the clay's color and texture are consistent.

After you've conditioned the clay, you can achieve an exciting range of colors and shades in much the same way you'd mix paints—by blending two or more colors together. The most important rule to keep in mind is to start with the lighter color of clay and add the darker color.

You'll use the different colors to create patterns. "Caning" is by far the most popular way to do this. With caning, you assemble rods or slabs of clay

in various colors to form a pattern; this is how polymer clay artists create intricate cross-sectional designs.

Start with a simple geometric pattern such as a checkerboard; then practice until you can repeat the desired result every time. To make a checkerboard cane, first flatten several pieces of clay, all conditioned to the same consistency, into rectangular sheets. (Start with equal portions of each color.) Use either a rolling pin or a pasta machine to flatten the clay sheets evenly. Stack the sheets on top of one another, alternating colors; then trim their ends even. Place the resulting striped loaf on end. Use a sharp, flat blade to cut slices that are the same thickness as the individual layers in the loaf. Assemble the checkerboard cane by placing the slices on top of one another, turning over every other one. Now cut slices from the end of the cane. You may use slices from all sorts of canes to create everything from

beads to the gorgeous projects on pages 32 and 113.

Finally, you'll need to bake your creation according to the manufacturer's directions. Metal and glass pans or baking sheets are fine, but the surface of the clay that comes in contact with them will have a shiny finish. To produce a matte finish, line the baking dish with a thin sheet of cardboard or oven parchment. Follow the manufacturer's instructions regarding temperature and baking time.

Working with Glass

The projects on pages 34-37, which are made by cutting strips of glass, include very detailed glass-cutting instructions for beginners and are very easy to make. Just read the tips that follow before you begin,

Cutting glass well—without cracking or chipping it—takes some practice. The best way to start is by going to your local window-glass store and purchasing a few pieces of broken glass. (Most stores have plenty on hand.) This window-strength glass, unlike most stained glass, is relatively thin, smooth surfaced, and easy to cut. Then use this scrap glass and the cutting instructions on pages 35-36 to practice scoring and breaking out glass strips. How can you tell when you've had enough practice? The pieces you cut will have even edges that are perpendicular to their flat surfaces—and your hands won't tremble with fear when you pick up the glass cutter!

Next, practice on some scrap stained glass from a stained-glass store or supplier. These colorful sheets often have textured surfaces; running your cutter smoothly over their lumps and bumps can be quite a challenge. Don't despair! The knack does come with time. If you get stuck, just ask a local stained-

glass artist if you can watch while he or she is at work. An hour or two spent with a proficient cutter is worth weeks of practice.

Take special care to wear safety glasses or goggles when you work, and cut your glass in an area with a smooth floor that can be thoroughly vacuumed. Glass-cutting creates thousands of tiny glass chips and splinters that love to hide in carpets and in the crevices in rough concrete! Never neglect cleaning up after each cutting session either, or the feet that pass through your work area (your own, your family's, and your pet's) may complain.

Working with Potter's Clay

The clay wind-chime project in this book (see pages 30-31) doesn't require much expertise. The clay medallions with which it's made do need to be fired in a kiln, however; just refer to this project's "Tips" section for advice on locating one. The only real problem with creating these clay chimes is that doing so may sweep you into a lifelong affair with clay itself. If you find yourself unable to resist the warmth and possibilities of this amazing material, consider taking an introductory course in ceramics. (Learning how to "hand-build"—or shape clay without a potter's wheel—is a good place to start.) In the meantime, you'll find that the clay wind-chime project instructions are very specific. If you're curious about clay-related topics that the instructions don't cover, by all means ask the potter who fires your work.

Chapter 2

Wind Chimes and Mobiles

Have you ever woken up on a late spring morning and just sat in bed, listening as the wind rustled and murmured through the tender new leaves? There's something soothing and harmonious about that wonderful rush of random music. The wind speaks and sings in so many voices. Everything it touches becomes an instrument: tall grasses on the prairie, deep canyons in the desert, sand on the beach. Wind is like the conductor for Nature's symphony.

Long ago, one of our ancestors must have decided to fuse the wind's musical talent with human ingenuity to create the first wind chime. Who knows when or where that was, what inspired that inventor, or what materials he or she used. Maybe that first chime was a simple arrangement of bamboo rods, dangled from a tree with strips of leather or hemp. Maybe it evolved from an early alarm system—objects suspended from a dwelling door, hung to startle trespassers and alert the people living inside. We can speculate, but in the end, we simply don't know.

Whoever crafted that first wind chime made a startling leap in creativity by doing so. Almost every other human-made musical instrument must be played by human hands or mouths. By contrast, the wind chime is played by Nature alone. When a breeze stirs a wind chime, the resulting music is a magical blend of human cunning and organic randomness.

Although Nature chooses the song that a wind chime sings, you choose the song's tone by selecting the materials with which you construct the chime. As you look through the wind chimes featured in this chapter, you'll immediately notice the tremendous variety of materials the designers used to make their projects. Between beads, glass, metal tubing, clay, tin votive candle holders, metal sheeting, flower pots, exotic coins, horseshoes, wood, and everyday hardware, it might seem that the designers have covered just about every wind chime component possible. Don't believe it for a minute!

If you put your mind to it, you'll find you can think of hundreds of other everyday items from which you can craft a wind chime. If you're like most folks, you probably have a ring-full of keys that don't seem to open any

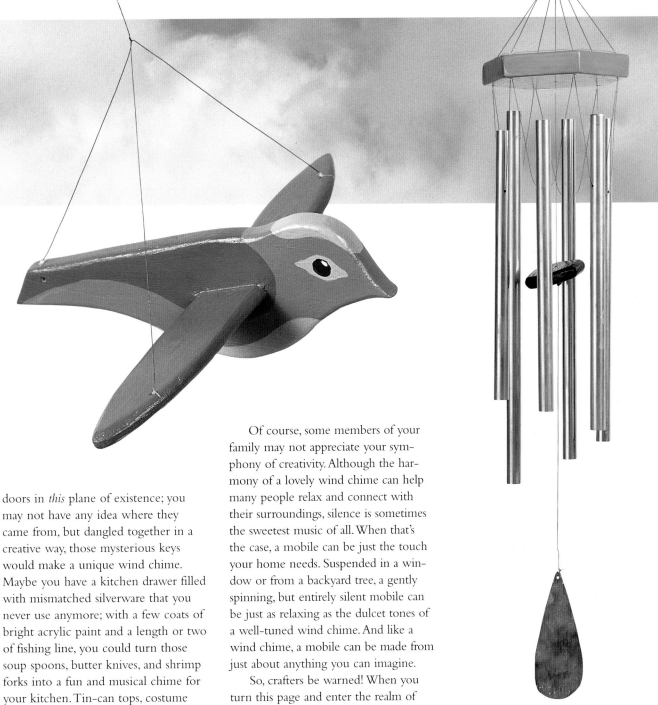

doors in *this* plane of existence; you may not have any idea where they came from, but dangled together in a creative way, those mysterious keys would make a unique wind chime. Maybe you have a kitchen drawer filled with mismatched silverware that you never use anymore; with a few coats of bright acrylic paint and a length or two of fishing line, you could turn those soup spoons, butter knives, and shrimp forks into a fun and musical chime for your kitchen. Tin-can tops, costume jewelry, old toys, cookie cutters, pens and pencils, golf balls, sea-shells, dried beans, pottery shards—you get the point! Read through this chapter for inspiration, look around your house for likely wind-chime parts, and soon you'll be filling every room in your home with the lively sound and song of your collaboration with the wind.

Of course, some members of your family may not appreciate your symphony of creativity. Although the harmony of a lovely wind chime can help many people relax and connect with their surroundings, silence is sometimes the sweetest music of all. When that's the case, a mobile can be just the touch your home needs. Suspended in a window or from a backyard tree, a gently spinning, but entirely silent mobile can be just as relaxing as the dulcet tones of a well-tuned wind chime. And like a wind chime, a mobile can be made from just about anything you can imagine.

So, crafters be warned! When you turn this page and enter the realm of wind chimes and mobiles, you enter a fertile field for the creative mind. You'll find yourself looking in downtown store windows and imagining the objects therein strung from monofilament. You'll stalk your local hardware store in search of exactly the right width of pipe for a silvery-sounding chime. You'll bankrupt your spare button jar borrowing its contents for your next innovation. Before long, your neighborhood will be filled with the sweet sounds and sight of the wind playing its newest instruments!

Musical *Wind Chime*

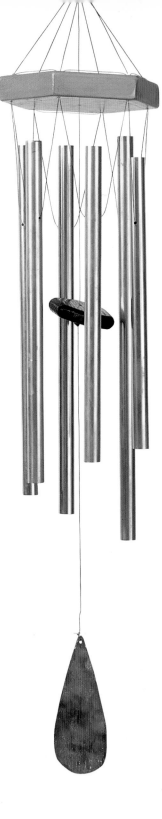

This amazing wind chime, designed by Eric Reiswig, is actually tuned to a minor pentatonic scale; the music it makes is exquisite. If you're musically inclined and would like to try making a chime that's tuned to an actual, selected pitch, you'll find instructions on pages 12-13.

Materials and Supplies

6 brass tubes, ½" diameter, 12" long

1 brass tube, ⅝" diameter, 4" long

1 piece of ¾" x 5" x 5" wood

1 piece of ½" x 2½" x 2½" wood

14' length of monofilament (fishing line)

1 ¼"-diameter bead

Paint or varnish

Plastic or metal split ring

Brass polish

Tools

Hacksaw or tubing cutter

Jigsaw or coping saw

Flat file

Small round file

Drill

¹⁄₁₆" drill bit

Paintbrush

Hammer

Pliers

Tin snips or strong scissors

Pencil

Ruler with millimeter
   increments

Tip

~For truly "musical" wind chimes like this one, you can use any tubing material that's uniformly thick and dense, as long each tube is the same diameter.

Instructions

1. Using a fine-toothed hacksaw or tubing cutter, cut the ½"-diameter brass tubes to the following lengths: 305 mm, 280 mm, 264 mm, 249 mm, 228 mm, and 216 mm.

2. Using the flat and round files, smooth the cut edges.

3. Measuring each tube from its cut end, mark the tubes as follows:

~On the 305 mm tube, mark at 69 mm.
~On the 280 mm tube, mark at 63 mm.
~On the 264 mm tube, mark at 59 mm.
~On the 249 mm tube, mark at 56 mm.
~On the 228 mm tube, mark at 51 mm.
~On the 216 mm tube, mark at 49 mm.

Note that these dimensions are based on marking each bar at 22.5% of its length.

4. To make two holes in each tube for a hanging line, drill a ¹⁄₁₆"-diameter hole right through the tube at the mark. Use a round file to deburr the holes.

5. To create a top plate for the chime, cut the 5" x 5" piece of wood into a hexagon. (The distance between any two opposing points should be 5".) Sand all the edges.

6. Drill seven ¹⁄₁₆"-diameter holes through the top plate: one through the center and one about ¼" in from each point.

7. To make the striker, cut the 2½" x 2½" piece of wood into a hexagon. (The distance between any two opposing points should be 2½".) Sand the edges to smooth them.

8. Drill a ¹⁄₁₆"-diameter hole through the center of the striker.

9. Apply paint or varnish to the top plate and striker and let the finish dry.

10. To make the teardrop-shaped windcatcher, start by using a hacksaw to split the ⅝"-diameter brass tubing lengthwise. Then, being careful not to cut yourself, use pliers to spread the tube open. Hammer the brass rectangle to flatten it.

11. Mark a teardrop shape on the flattened metal and use tin snips to cut it out. Deburr the edges with a file. Then drill a ¹⁄₁₆"-diameter hole through the teardrop, about ¼" down from its pointed end.

12. Tie one end of a 3'-long piece of monofilament to a metal or plastic split ring. Thread the other end through one of the corner holes in the top plate, back up through an adjacent hole,

through the split ring, and back down through the next adjacent hole. Repeat until the thread comes up through the last hole; then tie the free end of the line to the split ring. When you suspend the project by slipping the split ring over a hook, you should be able to level the top plate by adjusting the monofilament threaded through it.

13. To string each wind-chime tube, first cut a 16" length of monofilament and thread it through the two ¹⁄₁₆" holes in the longest (305 mm) tube. Then thread one end of the monofilament up through one corner hole in the top plate, and the other end up through a hole in an adjacent corner. (The tube will hang under one edge of the hexagon.) On the upper side of the top plate, tie the two ends of the monofilament with a square knot.

14. Repeat step 13 to attach the other six tubes, working from the longest to the shortest tube. (Hang the 280 mm tube next to the 305 mm tube, the 264 mm tube next to the 280 mm tube, and so on.) Try to suspend the tubes with their top ends, hanging holes, or center points aligned horizontally. Aligning the top ends makes an attractive arrangement, but aligning the center points will create a more uniform sound.

15. When all the tubes are in place, cut off the excess monofilament from each knot and slide each knot down into a corner hole to hide and protect it.

16. Cut a 22"-long piece of monofilament and tie one end to the split ring. Thread the other end down through the hole in the center of the top plate and then through the hole in the hexagonal striker. Tie the bead onto the monofilament below the striker, positioning it more or less level with

the centers of the tubes. The striker will now rest on top of the bead.

17. Tie the windcatcher to the bottom end of the monofilament, suspend the wind chime from a hook, and listen to its song.

Oriental Breeze *Wind Chime*

Have you ever wondered what to do with those pesky foreign coins that mysteriously appear in your change purse? Designer Diane Kuebitz combined her collection of oriental coins with chunks of jade to create an alluring wind chime. If you don't have a cache of foreign currency, you can make a similar chime with beads, buttons, faux exotic coins, and even everyday washers from your local hardware store.

Tools

Drill
⅛" drill bit
Scissors

Materials and Supplies

Dry tree branch or driftwood, about 1" thick and 1' long

Oriental coins, stones, beads, or trinkets with holes though their centers (see "Tip")

Wax-coated string

Tip

~Most gem stores carry attractive, inexpensive pre-drilled stones.

Instructions

1. Use a ⅛" drill bit to bore seven holes in the branch, spacing them about ¾" apart.

2. Cut five lengths of wax string at least three times as long as you'd like the final strands to be. (Diane's finished strands are about 7" long.)

3. Start by threading a coin, bead, stone, or trinket onto a string and tying it in place halfway down. Thread the lower half of the string back up through the object's hole. Add the other objects, threading the doubled string through their holes and knotting after each addition; this is how Diane

got the interesting "doubled" string effect on her chime. Repeat to thread objects onto all the strings. (Each completed strand will have two free ends of string at its top. Try to leave these free ends about 2" long.)

4. Thread one free end of each strand through each of the five interior holes on the tree branch. (The two outer holes are for the display string.)

5. Tie a bead (or other object) to the end of each string on the top of the branch—these will keep the strings from sliding back through the holes. Be sure to leave about ½" of string above each bead. Tie this ½"-end to the other string end and trim the excess string.

6. Finally, make the display loop. Cut a length of waxed string about three times as long as the branch. Thread a bead about halfway down the string and tie it in place. Then bring the lower half of the string up through the bead hole to create a doubled string. Thread the doubled string up through one of the two outer holes on the branch. As before, the bead will anchor the string in place. Thread the doubled string down through the top of the other outer hole. Thread a bead onto one end of the string; then tie the two string ends together.

7. Display and enjoy!

Bluebird Mobile

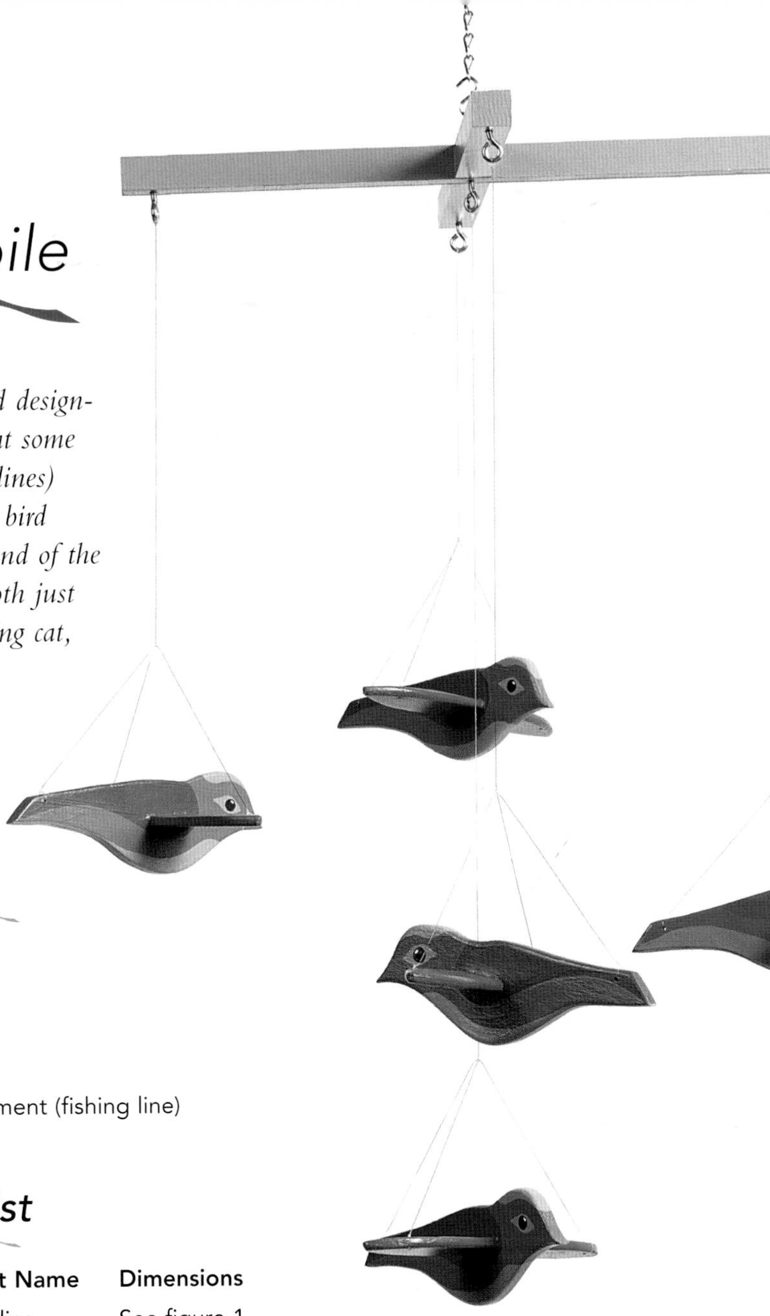

Robin Clark, a woodworker and renowned designer of innovative bluebird houses, knows that some properties (especially those with resident felines) don't make the best of nesting grounds for bird families. If you and your cat are equally fond of the little birds, Robin's mobile will suit you both just fine. A delicate breeze, rather than a stalking cat, will send this bluebird family into flight.

Tools

Tape measure
Pencil
Jigsaw
Coping saw
Drill
$\frac{1}{16}$" and $\frac{1}{4}$" drill bits
Wood chisel or sharp knife
Hammer
Square
Clamp
Paintbrushes

Supplies

Sandpaper
Wood glue
Wood filler
Exterior paints
10' of monofilament (fishing line)

Cutting List

Number	Part Name	Dimensions
5	Bodies	See figure 1
5	Wings	See figure 2

Lumber and Hardware

1 Piece of plywood, $\frac{1}{4}$" x 12" x 12"
1 Piece of plywood, $\frac{1}{8}$" x 12" x 12"
2 Pieces of $\frac{3}{4}$" x 1" trim, each 16" long
10 $1\frac{1}{4}$" brads
6 $\frac{1}{4}$" screw eyes
1 $\frac{1}{2}$" or $\frac{3}{4}$" screw eye or ceiling hook

Tips

~All the cuts in this project may be made with a coping saw, but a jigsaw or scroll saw will make some of your work easier.

~Feel free to substitute another type of wood for the plywood listed below.

Figure 1

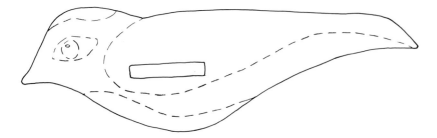

Figure 2

Instructions

1. Make a photocopy of figure 1, enlarging the body pattern until it is 7" long from the tip of the beak to the end of the tail. Also photocopy and enlarge figure 2; this enlarged wing pattern should also be 7" long.

2. Using a pencil and the enlarged photocopies, lightly trace five bird bodies onto the ¼"-thick plywood and five wings onto the ⅛"-thick plywood.

3. Cut out the wings and bodies with a jigsaw or coping saw.

4. Sand all the edges of the cut pieces to a smooth finish.

5. The rectangle in figure 1 indicates the slot into which the wing piece will fit. Using the enlarged body pattern again, transfer this marked area to each of the wooden bird bodies.

6. The easiest way to remove the wood inside these marked slot lines is to use a drill and sharp knife. First, use a ¼" drill bit to bore a series of connecting holes inside the marked slot lines, all the way through the body. To remove the remaining wood around each slot's edges, use a sharp knife.

7. Insert a wing into each body slot. To secure the wings in place, lightly hammer two brads through the upper edge of each body and through the wing. Fill any gaps with wood filler.

8. The two 16"-long pieces of molding that make up the mobile hanger are joined as shown in figure 3. To make this joint, each piece of molding must have a centered, ⅜"-deep, 1"-wide notch cut into its 1"-wide face. Begin by marking the cutting lines on the 1"-wide face of each piece, positioning each line 7½" from an end. Then

Figure 3

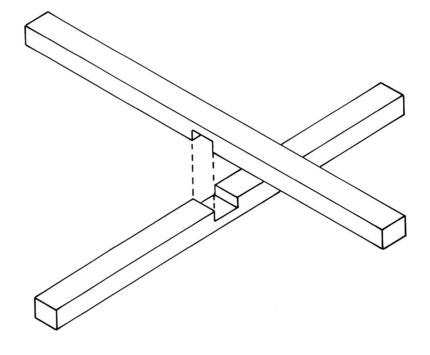

clamp the wood securely and use a coping saw to make a series of parallel ⅜"-deep cuts, very close together, between the marked lines. Remove the remaining wood with a wood chisel or sharp knife.

9. Glue the two pieces of molding together at the notches to form a half-lap joint, clamping the parts together until the glue dries.

10. Paint the birds and hanger pieces as you like, and allow the paint to dry thoroughly.

11. Attach one screw eye to the center of the top of the hanger and another to the center of the bottom.

12. On the bottom edge of each hanger arm, measure and mark a point ¾" in from each end. Attach a screw eye at each of these points.

13. To prepare holes in each bird for the monofilament, first mark a point on each end of the wing, 1" in from the wing tip and ¼" back from the wing's front edge. Also mark a point on the tail, ¾" from its tip and ¼" from its upper edge. Using a ¹⁄₁₆" drill bit, bore a hole at each marked point.

14. There are several ways to string the monofilament to each bird. One method is as follows: Start by threading a 25" length of monofilament through the top of a wing hole. Bring the line around the front of the wing and tie it to itself to secure it. Thread the other end of the line through the tail and then through the top of the other wing hole. Tie the line around the front of the wing again. Now use one finger to pull up two loops in the threaded line—one loop on each side of the body. (The line will form a pyramid with your fingers at the top and the

bird at the base.) Balance the bird by adjusting the length of the line on either side of the wing. Now tie another piece of monofilament (a "hanging" line) to the looped line, right at the balance point. Tie the hanging line to one of the screw eyes on the hanger. Repeat with the other birds, varying the heights at which they're suspended.

15. To suspend the mobile, tie one end of a piece of monofilament to the screw eye on top of the hanger and the other to a hook or screw eye in the ceiling.

Chicago, Illinois: the Windy City?

Around the world, people recognize the American Midwestern metropolis of Chicago by its designation, the Windy City. To the many folks who've had hats knocked off or skirts flipped over head by a good gust blowing off Lake Michigan, the origin of Chicago's nickname probably seems obvious; as it turns out, however, the city's bombastic promoters, rather than its blustery weather earned Chicago its gusty epithet.

Back in the early 1800s, Chicago sent hoards of very vocal advocates to the East Coast to proclaim the city's excellence as a place to invest. Upon hearing these proclamations, many people declared that Chicago's promoters were full of wind. A New York Sun editorial from the early 1890s cemented Chicago's reputation and nickname. The editor, Charles A. Dana, discussing the competition between New York City and Chicago to play host to the 1893 World's Columbian Exposition, warned against the "nonsensical claims of that windy city."

And ever since, people have been calling Chicago by that name. The city, has, however, been called by other nicknames. Some of these include:

**Pride of the Rustbelt ~ City of the Big Shoulders ~ City in a Garden ~ Hog Butcher to the World ~
"I Will" City ~ Gem of the Prairie ~ Packingtown ~ Second City**

Falling Flowers *Wind Chime*

Avid gardeners will love this floral wind chime, which lends a new twist—an upside-down one!—to container gardening. Mike Durkin, the creative woodworker who designed this project, made his own wind-chime tubes. If you'd like to do the same, just refer to the instructions on pages 12-13.

Tools

Tape measure

Pencil

Compass

Jigsaw or coping saw

Clamps

Paintbrushes

Drill

¹⁄₁₆" and ⅛" drill bits

Materials & Supplies

Sandpaper

Exterior paints

8' length of monofilament (fishing line)

5 wind-chime tubes in varying lengths (see "Tips")

7' length of black nylon string

Paper or plastic cup, with a bottom approx. 2" in diameter

Small box of plaster of Paris

Small clay watering pitcher or other decorative weight

Clay or plastic flowerpot, 4" in diameter

Lumber and Hardware

Number		
1	Pine 1 x 4, 24" long	
17	¼" screw eyes	
1	Small nut or flat metal washer	
1	Plastic or metal split ring	
1	½" or ¾" screw eye	

Tip

~Plaster of Paris is available at hardware and building-supply stores.

Cutting List

Number	Part Name	Dimensions
1	Wooden circle	¾" x 3" diameter
5	Tulips	see figure 1

Instructions

1. Photocopy the flower pattern in figure 1, enlarging it until the flower is 2¼" wide.

2. Transfer the enlarged pattern, five times, to the 1 x 4 stock. Also mark a 3"-diameter circle on this stock.

3. Using a coping saw or jigsaw, cut out the five flowers and the wooden circle. Smooth the edges of all six pieces by sanding them well.

4. Using exterior paints, paint the flowers and the wooden circle as desired.

5. Mark the center points on both faces of the wooden circle and insert a small screw eye at each mark. (You may need to use a ⅟₁₆" drill bit to drill small pilot holes for the screw-eye threads.) Tie a 12" length of monofilament to the screw eye in the upper face of the circle, and a 24" length to the screw eye in the bottom face.

6. On the bottom face of the circle, mark five equidistant points in a circle, close to the rim. Insert a small screw eye at each mark. (The wind-chime tubes will be suspended from these.)

7. Tie a 12" length of monofilament to one of the five screw eyes in the bottom face of the circle. Thread one wind-chime tube onto the line; then tie the other end of the line to the next screw eye. Working around the circle of screw eyes, repeat this step with four more 12" lengths of monofilament and four more wind-chime tubes. Make sure that the tops of the tubes are even.

8. Now, working on the bottom face of the circle again, insert a screw eye

between each of the five screw eyes that you just threaded. These new screw eyes should be positioned directly above the wind-chime tubes hanging beneath.

9. To each of the screw eyes you just inserted, tie a 14" to 16" length of nylon string. Then thread each of these strings through the wind-chime tube suspended beneath it.

10. At the bottom of each piece of dark string, tie a small screw eye. Make sure to tie each one fairly close to the bottom of the wind-chime tube.

11. Insert each of the dangling screw eyes into the bottom of a wooden flower.

12. To make the ringer circle that will strike the wind-chime tubes, first mix a small amount of plaster of Paris, following the manufacturer's directions. Then pour about ¼" of liquid plaster into a paper or plastic cup. Let the plaster dry, remove the cup, and use a ⅛" drill bit to drill a small hole through the center of the plaster circle.

13. Slide the plaster ringer circle onto the 24" length of monofilament extending from the bottom center of the wooden circle, and position the ringer halfway down among the wind-chime tubes. To hold it in place, tie a small nut or washer just beneath it.

14. At the end of the 24" monofilament, tie a decorative weight such as the miniature clay watering can used in this project.

15. To attach the 4"-diameter flower pot at the top of the wind chime, simply turn the pot upside down and thread the monofilament that extends from the upper face of the wooden cir-

Figure 1

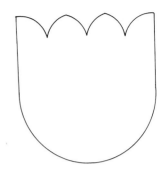

cle through the hole in the bottom of the pot. (If your pot lacks a hole, just drill one with a ⅛" drill bit.) When you lift the chime by this line, the wooden disc will pull up against the interior circumference of the pot.

16. Tie a plastic or metal split ring to the monofilament at the top of the wind chime and suspend it from a ½" or ¾" screw eye or hook.

Impressed Clay *Wind Chime*

You don't need to be a professional potter to make these musical chimes. In fact, this project—designed by potter Lee Davis—is a great one for people who have always loved the warmth and beauty of clay but who have never had the opportunity to work with it before.

Tools

Rolling pin

Small paintbrush

Respirator or dust mask

Rubber gloves

Materials and Supplies

Newspaper

3 to 5 pounds of clay (see "Tips")

2 yardsticks or thin strips of wood

Wooden matchsticks

Short length of ¼"-diameter dowel, or any thin, tubular object

Iron oxide (see "Tips")

10' of monofilament fishing line (15-pound)

10" to 12" of heavy wire or nylon cord

Tips

~Don't despair if you don't own a kiln (the "oven" in which potter's clay is baked to harden it). Potters are often generous souls and for a small fee, many will add your work to their own when they "fire" a kilnload of ware. You might also try a university ceramics department or one of the commercial pottery-painting stores that have become so popular in recent years.

~Many different clays are available. Purchase any light-colored clay "body" for this project, but be sure that it's a "high-firing" clay—above cone 5. Chimes made with low-fire clays won't make the same wonder-ful music! Be sure to find out what your clay's "cone firing range" is when you buy it. You (or the person who fires your clay) will need to know this before the clay is placed in a kiln.

~As you can see in the photo, the clay medallions that make up this wind chime have been stamped (or impressed). The instructions that follow will walk you through how to make your own clay stamps, but you can also create textures and shapes in the medallions by pressing and shaping their surfaces with any objects you like—including bits of textured wood, sea shells, or tools.

~Iron-oxide powder can be purchased from any clay supplier. It's sold by the pound and is usually very inexpensive.

~If you don't own a good respirator, work outdoors and set up a fan to blow any clay or iron-oxide particles away from you.

Instructions

1. To make the clay stamps that are used to impress the medallions, start by gathering natural objects such as berries, pine needles, leaves, and nuts.

2. Place the natural objects on a sheet of newspaper. Then press a ball of clay, about 1" to 1½" in diameter firmly down on top of each one. Pinch up a small bit of clay on the top surface of each piece to form a handle.

3. Turn each stamp over and carefully remove the natural object.

4. When the clay stamps you've just made are completely dry, they should be "bisque fired" in a kiln. (Dry clay that hasn't been fired is very fragile.) Bisque firing, because it takes place at temperatures too low to melt all the silica in the clay, will leave your stamps somewhat porous and will therefore make them easier to use. If you have a kiln, bisque fire the stamps now. If you don't own a kiln, you'll need to find someone who can bisque fire them for you.

5. To begin making the medallions and beads for your wind chime, first cover a flat work surface with one sheet of newspaper.

6. Place two yardsticks or thin strips of wood on the newspaper, parallel to each other and 6" apart.

7. On a separate sheet of newspaper, roll out several coils of clay, each about the length and thickness of your thumb, and several more about 6" long and as thick as your little finger. Also roll several balls of clay, each about 1" in diameter, and several small balls about ½" in diameter.

8. Using a wooden matchstick, punch a small hole through the center of each ½"-diameter ball. Set these balls aside.

9. Shape the 6"-long coils into doughnuts and press the clay together at the seams. Then cover them with a single sheet of newspaper and roll them out by running a rolling pin back and forth across the sticks. (The sticks will guarantee that all the clay medallions are flattened to an equal thickness.)

10. Remove the yardsticks, peel off the top layer of newspaper, and use clay stamps to impress the upper surfaces of the medallions. Replace the sheet of newspaper when you're finished.

11. Grip the entire newspaper-and-clay "sandwich" at its top edge and carefully flip it over. Then peel off the top layer of paper.

12. Using a matchstick again, punch a small hole through each piece.

13. Repeat these steps until you've made all the smaller clay medallions, but reserve some clay for the large medallion at the top of the wind chime.

14. Allow the medallions and the ½"-diameter balls that you made in step 7 to dry uncovered.

15. To make the large clay medallion at the top of the chime, use the same rolling-pin technique, but start out with a thick pancake-shaped piece of clay about 6" in diameter. After rolling this medallion out, use a short length of ¼"-diameter dowel to punch two holes at its top, spacing them about ¼" from the upper edge. Also use a matchstick to punch six evenly spaced, smaller holes along the bottom edge.

16. When all the clay shapes are dry, mix together about 2 to 3 tablespoons of iron oxide and 1 cup of water. (Wear a respirator and rubber gloves when you do this. Inhaling or ingesting iron oxide isn't a good idea, and the liquid mixture will stain whatever it touches.) Then brush both sides of the medallions and a few of the small balls with this mixture. Lee left some of the balls uncoated; they're the white ones in his wind chime.

17. When the iron oxide has dried, turn each medallion so that its impressed side is face up. Wearing your respirator and gloves, use fine steel wool to remove the excess iron oxide from the raised portions of the clay. The iron oxide remaining in the impressions will turn these lower areas reddish brown when the clay is fired.

18. Fire the clay to maturity. (If someone else will be doing the firing for you, be sure to give them the firing range of your clay and tell them that you'd like the clay fired to maturity.)

19. To assemble the fired clay pieces, first cut six lengths of monofilament, each about 40" long, and tie a small fired ball of clay to one end of each length.

20. Thread each line through one of the six small holes in the large clay medallion that will rest at the top of your wind chime. The clay ball on the end of each line will act as a "stop" at the hole.

21. Using the project photo as a guide, thread the clay shapes and balls onto the lengths of monofilament.

22. Make a hanger for your finished wind chime by tying a short length of sturdy wire or nylon cord though the two holes in the large medallion.

Rainbow Wind Chime

This polymer-clay wind chime, designed by Diane Kuebitz, may not come with a pot of gold, but its rainbowlike colors and musical tones will certainly enliven your porch or backyard. It's also a perfect first project for folks who have never worked with polymer clay before.

Tools

Tape measure

Slicing blade or single-edged razor blade

Rolling pin or pasta machine

Piercing tool or thin wooden dowel

Large, ovenproof glass baking dish

Conventional oven

Oven thermometer

Timer

Tips

~If you can't find wind-chime tubes at a craft store, turn to pages 12-13 for instructions on making your own.

~For basic instructions on working with polymer clay, refer to pages 18-19.

Materials and Supplies

1 block each of red, orange, yellow, green, blue, and purple polymer clay

½ block of black polymer clay

5 pieces of ¼"-diameter copper tubing, each approximately ¼" long

Leather string, approximately 48" long

3 wind-chime tubes

Clear acrylic craft sealer spray

Instructions

1. To create the ¼"-thick rainbow slab that forms the main portion of this wind chime, first cut a piece of clay from each colored block except the black one.

2. Using your rolling pin or pasta machine, roll out each piece of clay until it's about ¼" thick.

3. Stack the slabs, in any order you like, and press them together to form a loaf shape. You'll slice the "building blocks" of your design from this multi-colored clay loaf. (Depending on how you arrange the slabs in your stack, slicing through the loaf can result in

many different patterns, including parquet and checkerboard.)

4. Using your slicing blade or a single-edged razor blade, cut vertical slices of clay from the loaf.

5. Set the slices flat on your work surface. Using the project photo as a guide, cut each slice to the shape desired; then arrange them edge-to-edge to form a large slab and press their edges together to join them.

6. To make a black border for the rainbow slab you've created, first shape some of the black clay into a fairly thin strip, making the strip as wide as the rainbow slab is thick. Then wrap this black strip around the exterior edge of the rainbow slab, pressing it in place as you do.

7. As you can see in the project photo, the designer has added a number of embellishments by cutting thin slices from creatively formed clay canes. If you'd like to make similar decorations, first refer to the cane-making instructions on pages 18-19. Then cut very thin slices from the canes and press them in place on the front and back of the rainbow slab.

8. The wind-chime tubes are suspended from pieces of leather string that run through holes in the rainbow slab. Use short lengths of copper tubing to punch these holes in the large slab. Also punch two holes at the top of the slab for the leather-string hanger. (Don't leave the pieces of tubing in the holes; you must bake the clay before reinserting them.)

9. To make the decorative shapes that are strung above the wind-chime tubes, cut and shape slices from a variety of canes, or roll clay balls made up of different colored clays. Use a piercing tool or thin wooden dowel to pierce a hole in each clay shape.

10. Place the rainbow slab and other clay shapes in a large, ovenproof glass baking dish. Bake the clay according to the clay manufacturer's directions.

11. After the clay has cooled, insert the five lengths of copper tubing into the holes in the rainbow slab.

12. Cut the 48" length of string into four equal lengths. Assemble the wind-chime tubes and decorative clay shapes on three of these lengths, tying knots to prevent the clay shapes from slipping downward. Then, using the project photo as a guide, tie the strings through the holes in the rainbow slab, trimming them as desired to vary the heights at which the wind-chime tubes hang.

13. To make a hanger, thread the fourth length of leather string through the two tubes in the holes at the top of the rainbow slab. Tie this string securely.

14. Spray the clay portions of the project with clear acrylic craft sealer to protect them and to make them shiny.

Wind Words

We've all heard that each of the various Eskimo languages has at least a hundred words to describe snow, right? Well, English may not have a quite one hundred words for wind, but it certainly has more than you might think. Take a look at the following list:

blast ~ blow ~ bluster ~ breeze ~ chinook ~ crosswind ~ draft ~ easterly ~ fohn (or foehn) ~ gale ~ gust ~ harmattan ~ head wind ~ monsoon ~ norther (or northerly) ~ nor'wester (or northwester) ~ simoom (also simoon or samiel) ~ sou'easter (southeaster) ~ sou'wester (or southwester) ~ squall ~ wester (or west wind) ~ zephyr ~

Japanese has more than a few words to describe wind, too. You're probably familiar with one of them already—the word "kamikaze" (or "divine wind"). Like vengeful gales from the heavens, these famous Japanese pilots of WW II swept down in their planes, crashing them into their targets below.

Other Japanese wind words include:

agensutouindo ~ gyakufuu ~ higashikaze ~ higashiyori ~ hokufuu ~ ichijin ~ kanpuu ~ karakaze ~ kaze ~ kazeatori ~ kitakaze ~ kitaoroshi ~ kitayori ~ kochi ~ kogarashi ~ kyoufuu ~ junbuu ~ makaze ~ minamikaze ~ mukaikaze ~ nanpuu ~ nan'yori ~ nishikaze ~ oroshi ~ oufuu ~ shimakaze ~ soyokaze ~ takuetsufuu ~ toufuu ~ yokaze ~ yokokaze

Sun and Sky *Wind Chime*

Christi Hensley has designed a chime that celebrates the sun as well as the wind. Sunshine streaming through panels of painted glass turns this gorgeous and unique project into a stunning show of sound and colored light.

Materials and Supplies

Copper sheeting, approximately 6" x 12"

4' to 6' of heavy-gauge copper wire

Scrap of wood, at least 1' x 1' and 1" thick

1' of ¼"-diameter copper tubing

Rags

Fine-gauge steel wool

Clear, single-strength window glass (see "Tips")

Glass beads in colors of your choice (see "Tips")

Acrylic paint stain for glass in colors of your choice (see "Tips")

Muriatic acid (optional; see "Tips")

Clear acrylic craft sealer spray

Sewing-machine oil

Small tin can

Tools

Tape measure

Marker

Protective gloves

Tin snips

Hammer

Chisel

Metal file

Pliers

Wire cutters

Safety glasses

Thick straightedge or thin strip of wood

Glass cutter

Drill

⅛" drill bit for glass or tile

⅛" split-point drill bit

Large nail

Hacksaw or pipe cutter

Paintbrushes

Tips

~Metal and glass can cause nasty cuts, so wear heavy gloves as you work. Also wear safety glasses when you cut and drill the glass for this project.

~Many craft stores carry acrylic paint stains for glass.

~Christi used clear window glass that she painted herself. Feel free to use stained glass strips instead.

~You'll find stained glass at stained-glass stores. It's usually sold by the square foot, but some stores also sell "scrap glass"—inexpensive left-over strips that will suit your needs very well. This project requires about 1 square foot, but buy a bit more—you'll break a few pieces as you practice cutting and drilling it!

~Learning to cut glass isn't terribly difficult, but you may want to practice on clear window glass first, as it's less expensive than stained glass. If you'd rather skip this learning process entirely, just have your glass strips cut at the store.

~Christi used muriatic acid to give the copper sheeting an attractive weathered look, a process described in steps 9 and 10; these steps are strictly optional. Muriatic acid can be very dangerous, and you simply cannot be careful enough when working with it. If you choose to use this acid, wear long pants, a long-sleeved shirt, rubber gloves, and safety goggles. Follow the manufacturer's instructions to the letter. Finally, keep muriatic acid far out of the reach of children.

Instructions

Making the Copper Pieces

1. Put on your gloves and cut one 5½" x 7¾" rectangle from the copper sheeting with a pair of tin snips.

2. Mark a 2½" x 4" rectangle in the center of the copper rectangle. (This marked rectangle represents the "window" into which the glass panel will fit.) With the chisel and hammer, make a cut in the center of the marked window. Using this cut as a starting point and working with tin snips, cut away a centered 1" x 3¼" rectangle of copper from the interior of the marked window.

3. To make the copper prongs that will hold the glass in place, use your tin snips to make a series of straight cuts along the interior edges of the rectangular opening. These cuts should extend to the marked window outline. (You'll fold these cut copper prongs around the edges of the glass once the glass is in place.) Smooth any sharp edges with a metal file.

4. Place the rectangle of copper on top of a piece of scrap wood. Use the hammer and nail to punch a series of holes along one short end of the rectangle, about ¼" from its edge; the chimes will dangle from these holes. The number of chimes you plan to suspend will determine the number of holes needed. Christi punched ten holes and hung seven chimes; the empty holes add extra interest.

5. Punch two to four holes at the other short end of the rectangle. You'll use the two outer holes for the chime's display wire.

6. From the copper sheeting, cut a semicircle with a diameter of about 5"; this piece will be the windcatcher. Place the piece on top of the scrap wood and use a nail and hammer to punch a centered hole about ¼" from the semicircle's straight edge. Punch a second hole directly opposite the first about ¼" from the semicircle's curved edge.

7. Cut the copper tubing into two 6" pieces with a hacksaw or a pipe cutter.

8. Use a ⅛" split-point drill bit to bore a hole about ½" from one end of each tube, piercing both sides of the tubing.

9. Cure the copper pieces with muriatic acid, carefully following the manufacturer's directions. It's best to perform this task outdoors, wearing safety goggles and protective rubber gloves. Use an old paintbrush to coat the copper pieces with diluted muriatic acid solution (see the manufacturer's instructions for details on diluting). You may want to experiment with scrap pieces of copper to become familiar with the process. Allow the copper to dry completely; then apply several more coats of solution until you're satisfied with the result.

10. Carefully rinse the copper pieces with water and let them dry. Then spray the pieces with a clear acrylic craft sealer to prevent the blue-green surface from rubbing off.

Cutting the Glass

11. Now you must cut four 1½" x 5" strips of glass and one 3" x 4¼" panel of glass. To prepare the glass for cutting, cover a flat work surface with several sheets of newspaper and set your sheet of glass down on top of the paper (if the glass has a shiny side, make sure it's facing up). Wipe the glass clean with a paper towel or rag. Put on safety goggles and gloves. Place a small amount of fine-gauge steel wool in an empty tin can, and dampen it with sewing-machine oil.

12. Place a thick straightedge or thin, straight-edged piece of wood down flat on the glass, leaving a 1½"-wide strip of glass exposed on the right-hand side (reverse this direction if you're left-handed). Hold the straightedge firmly in place with your left hand (don't press down too hard or the glass will break). Hold the cutter in your right hand, almost as if it were a pen, with your index finger on the flat portion of the handle and your thumb underneath. To lubricate the small, circular cutting "blade" at the end of the cutter, dab it a few times against the oil-soaked steel wool.

13. You don't actually "cut" the glass with a glass cutter; instead, you use the cutter to "score" the glass, creating a tiny, almost invisible fracture line. Then you use your hands to break the glass along the scored line. To start, place the cutter at the top edge of the glass, right next to the straightedge. Hold the cutter almost upright, tilting it slightly towards you but making sure that the handle is perfectly vertical from left to right.

14. Using the straightedge as a guide for the cutter, pull the cutter down the glass surface in one, smooth, relatively fast motion, pressing down firmly, as if you were using chalk to make a long line on the chalkboard. Don't stop until the cutter drops off the bottom edge of the glass; pausing midway will cause an uneven break. Try to keep the cutter from tilting to the left or right. If you see any splinters of glass forming in the wake of the cutter, you're pressing down too hard.

15. To "break out" the strip of glass you've scored, move the glass to the edge of the work surface, aligning the scored line with the edge of the work surface and allowing the strip to protrude into space. Hold the straightedge on top of the glass, right next to the score line, so the extra glass is "sandwiched" firmly between the straightedge and work surface. Then use your free hand to break the free-hanging strip of glass off by pulling down and away from the work surface.

16. Repeat steps 12 through 15 to cut the 1½"-wide strip to 5" in length. Also cut three more glass strips the same size, and a 3" x 4¼" glass rectangle.

17. With an electric drill and glass-cutting bit, gently bore a small hole at the top of each of the glass strips (don't bore a hole in the panel intended for the window). Apply pressure gradually, or you'll crack the glass. Wear safety goggles and gloves while you're drilling.

18. Paint the clear glass strips with acrylic paints, following the manufacturer's directions. Allow the paint to dry completely before assembling the chime. To recreate Christi's design, use blue and orange stain and refer to the photograph as a guide.

Assembling the Wind Chime

19. Using pliers, bend back a pair of prongs along each interior edge of the copper rectangle and flatten them down. These will serve only as decorative elements on the "back" surface of the copper rectangle. Bend the remaining prongs toward the "front" surface of the rectangle and flatten them down. The window outline that you marked in step 2 should now be entirely open. Place the glass panel in this opening; then bend some of the front prongs around the glass to hold it in place. Leave the other front prongs as flattened decorative elements.

20. To make the display hanger, cut a 22" length of copper wire and thread it through one of the outer holes at the top of the copper rectangle. Pull the wire so that the ends are uneven, making one side a few inches shorter than the other. Wrap the shorter side around the longer side of the wire. (The end should be secured by wrapping it against the longer side of the wire, and should not stick out.) Thread the loose end (the longer side of the wire) through the other hole, and wrap the wire around itself on the other side to secure the hanging wire.

21. Cut five lengths of copper wire varying in length from 3" to 5".

22. Thread one end of each wire through the hole of a glass strip, securing it by wrapping the copper wire around itself at the top of the glass. Then thread the other end of the wire through a hole in the bottom of the copper rectangle, again securing it by wrapping it around itself. Repeat this process for all of the glass strips.

23. Cut two 6" to 8" lengths of copper wire for each of the copper tubes. Repeat the steps used to hang the glass strips.

24. Cut a piece of copper wire about 17" long to hang the copper windcatcher. Thread the wire through the hole in the bottom of the copper rectangle and secure it. Thread several glass beads onto the other end of the wire, place them about halfway up the wire, and tie a knot directly below them to keep them in place. Thread the end of the copper wire through the hole in the flat edge of the windcatcher and secure the wire by wrapping it around itself several times.

25. Cut a 2" to 3" length of wire for the beads at the bottom of the windcatcher. Thread about ½" of the wire through the hole at the bottom (the curved side) of the windcatcher. Hook the wire sharply on the other side to secure it. Thread several beads onto the remaining wire; then hook the other end sharply, pressing it firmly up against the beads to keep them from falling off.

26. Display your chime in a sunny, slightly breezy spot. (Keep in mind that strong breezes might crack or break the glass.)

Tin and Glass Wind Chime

A variation on the last project, Christi Hensley used leftover scraps of roofing tin in this gorgeous wind chime. The instructions are abbreviated; just refer to pages 35-36 for more details and for lists of basic tools, materials, and supplies.

Materials and Supplies

Roofing tin or sheet metal, approximately 24" x 24"

Piece of beach glass or large glass fragment (optional)

5' of heavy-gauge aluminum wire

10' of light-gauge aluminum wire

Glass beads as desired

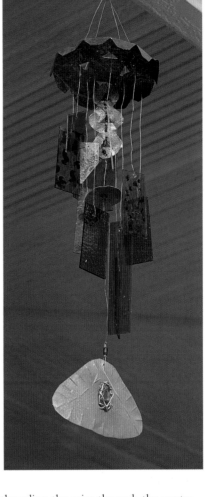

Instructions

1. Cut a 9" circle from the tin. Then, using the photo as a guide, cut a series of scallops around the edge of the circle.

2. To make the four triangular cutouts in this circle, use a hammer and chisel, pounding the chisel through the tin to create each straight cut.

3. Punch a hole through the circle's center with a hammer and nail. Then punch four equally spaced holes around the circumference, about 1" in from the cut scallops, for the four hanger wires. Add nine more holes, scattering them evenly over the circle's surface, but avoiding the scalloped areas.

4. With a file, smooth the rough edges. Then hammer out any dents. Using pliers, bend the scallops down . The flat portion of the circle should now be about 7" in diameter.

5. Cut the windcatcher piece from the tin. To impress lines into it, position

a chisel on the metal and tap it lightly with a hammer. Be careful not to strike the chisel too hard, or you'll cut through the tin.

6. To add a piece of beach glass to the windcatcher, first trace the outline of the glass onto the tin. Then use the traced lines to cut a hole. Punch a series of small holes around the hole you just cut. Place the beach glass in the large hole and secure it by weaving heavy-gauge wire in and out of the smaller holes. Then hammer out any unwanted dents and smooth away any rough edges.

7. Using the photo as a guide, cut two additional pieces of tin to hang on the windcatcher wire.

8. Assemble the windcatcher and two tin pieces on light-gauge wire, adding glass beads as desired. To hold the beads and tin in place, just twist the wire beneath them or make loose knots in it. Suspend the assembled strand by

threading the wire through the center hole in the scalloped tin circle.

9. Make a hanger for the chimes by cutting two pieces of heavy-gauge wire, each 18" long. Holding the two pieces together, fold them in half and, tie a 4" length of heavy-gauge wire around them, about 2" down from the folded ends. Thread each of the four free ends through a hole in the scalloped circle. Bend each wire end to hold it in place against the bottom of the circle.

10. Read steps 11-18 on pages 35-36. Then cut, drill holes in, and paint 13 pieces of window glass, each approximately 2" wide. (You may cut stained glass strips instead, or combine painted glass and stained glass as Christi has.) Attach a length of light-gauge wire to each piece and suspend the wires from the holes in the scalloped circle.

Winter Tree Mobile

Virginia Boegli designed this lovely, delicate mobile for indoor use or for display in a covered porch area. Although the paper mache birds and leaves are durable (even a fall isn't likely to harm them), they aren't waterproof, and a strong wind will tangle the mobile or break the twigs.

Materials and Supplies

24 ounces of prepared cellulose wallpaper paste

12 ounces of white craft glue

2 pieces of flexible plastic sheeting, each 12" x 14" (see "Tips")

30 sheets of white tissue paper

3 water balloons

3 pieces of string, each 36" to 48" long

Newspapers

3 tree branches with twigs, each 15" to 20" long (see "Tips")

30 small green leaves

Small scrap of corrugated cardboard

Drinking glass or cup

Acrylic paints

Small roll of 28-gauge black wire

30 feet of 10-pound monofilament (fishing line)

10 black fishing swivels (size #10 or #12, safety-pin type)

5 black fishing swivels (size #10, cross-line type)

Tips

~You'll find medium-thick plastic sheeting, just like the plastic used to winterize windows, at any hardware store.

~Select branches with interesting twig arrangements. Virginia used old-growth lilac branches.

Tools

2" or 3" pastry brush

1 large margarine tub or similar plastic container with lid

Paper clip

Tape measure

Pruning or kitchen shears

Small sharp scissors

Hot-melt glue gun

Push pin

Watercolor brush

Wire cutters or an old pair of scissors

Small needlenose pliers

Instructions

1. Using the pastry brush as a mixer, combine the wallpaper paste and craft glue in a plastic tub.

2. Spread out one piece of plastic sheeting on a flat work surface. Then use the pastry brush to spread a thin layer of the paste mixture over it. Cut a piece of tissue paper to a size slightly smaller than the sheeting and spread the paper over the glue-covered sheeting.

3. Apply a thin coat of paste over the tissue. Then place another sheet of tissue on top. Repeat once more so that three layers of tissue paper are pasted onto the sheeting.

4. Apply a final coat of paste to the top layer of the tissue mache and arrange the leaves on the paste, leaving some space around each one. When you cut the leaves apart, you'll leave a narrow mache border around each one and a small mache tab at each stem end.

5. Cover the leaves with three more layers of paste and tissue. Then set the sheet aside to dry for two days.

6. On the second piece of plastic sheeting, build up six layers of tissue and paste. Set this sheet of mache aside to dry for two days.

7. Blow up a water balloon to the desired size for a bird body (don't put any water in it). Tie the balloon securely to close it.

8. Unbend the center of a paper clip to make a hook at each end. Spear the knotted end of the balloon with one hook and tie a piece of string to the other. Then use the string to suspend the hooked balloon over your work surface. (The knotted end will eventually become the bird's mouth.)

9. Place several sheets of newspaper under the balloon. Then tear a sheet of tissue (don't use scissors here) into pieces that are approximately 2" x 2". Set the pieces to one side of the newspaper, and the tub of paste mixture and the pastry brush on the other side.

10. Use one hand to grasp the balloon at its top. With the pastry brush held in your other hand, apply a layer of paste to the balloon.

11. With the damp (not dripping) brush, pick up a piece of tissue, being careful not to get any of the other pieces wet, transfer it to the balloon, and brush it down flat. Working from the bottom of the balloon upward, apply at least four overlapping layers of tissue and paste over the entire surface except for the knotted end.

12. Hang the bird body in a safe place and allow it to dry for two days. Repeat steps 7 to 11 to make two more bird bodies. Let these dry as well.

13. Using sharp pruning shears or kitchen shears, trim away any very small and brittle twigs on the three branches. Then trim the remaining portions to provide an interesting shape for your mobile.

14. Carefully peel the plastic sheeting away from the layered sheet of leaves and tissue paper. If the underside of the paper mache is still damp, turn the paper damp side up and allow it to dry for another day.

15. When the sheet is completely dry, carefully cut out each leaf, leaving a narrow margin of mache around its edges and a small mache tab at the stem end (you'll use this tab to hang the leaf).

16. Set each leaf, one by one, on a scrap of cardboard and make a hole in the tab by piercing the tab with a push pin.

17. Peel away the plastic sheeting from the second sheet of mache. Then, using figures 1, 2, and 3 as guides, trace and cut out three 2½"-long tails, six 1"-long beak pieces, and three 1"-long "feet."

18. Plug in your glue gun and allow it to heat up. Remove the hook from one of the bird bodies and rest the body on the rim of a glass or cup, with the tummy over the opening.

Figure 2

Beak

Figure 3

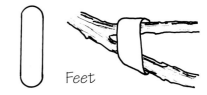

Feet

Figure 1

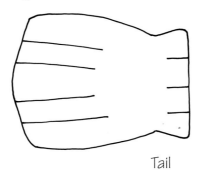

Tail

19. Cut the short and long slits in the mache tails. Bend up the short tabs on one tail, and position the tail on the bird body. Shape the short tabs to the curve of the body, cutting deeper slits if necessary. Then apply hot glue to the tabs and press them in place on the body for ten seconds.

20. Pull gently on the balloon knot —just enough to allow you to snip a small hole in the balloon, right behind the knot. The balloon may collapse immediately, pulling itself away from the paper mache. If it doesn't, be patient. If you listen closely, you'll hear little snaps as the balloon gradually pulls free by itself. When the balloon is free, carefully remove it from the paper mache bird body.

21. To shape an upper and lower beak, bend the tabs on one piece to the inside and, on the other piece, to the outside. Position the beak pieces on the bird body and shape the tabs just as you did the tail tabs. Then hot glue the beak pieces in place.

22. Repeat steps 18 to 21 to assemble the other two birds.

23. Using a watercolor brush and acrylic paints, paint the bird bodies as desired. Be careful not to get the birds too wet as you do this. Also paint the three feet black and allow them to dry.

24. Cut a piece of monofilament and make a long loop in one end; this will serve as a temporary branch hanger as you work. Attach the other end of the monofilament to a ceiling hook or beam. Slip the loop over the branch that you'd like to have at the top of your mobile and shift the branch until you find the point at which it will balance properly.

25. Choose a spot for one bird on the butt end of the branch. (The crotch between two branches is perfect because it provides more surface area for attaching a foot piece.)

26. Curl one black foot around the branch (or branches) and hot glue it in position. Then position the bird on the foot and hot glue it in place. (Be sure to hold it for at least ten seconds as the glue sets.) That end of the branch will dip down, but don't adjust it yet.

27. Repeat steps 24, 25, and 26 to suspend the other two branches and attach the remaining two birds.

28. Open the "safety-pin" end of a fishing-line swivel, slip it through the hole in a leaf tab, and snap the swivel closed. With wire cutters or old scissors, cut a 3" length of black wire and slip it through the small looped end of the swivel. Center the wire in the swivel loop and then attach the swivel near the end of a twig on one of the branches by wrapping the wire around the twig. Use your needlenose pliers to twist the wire ends together tightly and neatly. Repeat to attach all the leaves to the three branches.

29. Starting with the uppermost branch, slide the temporary monofilament loop along the branch as necessary to adjust the balance point for maximum motion. Mark the balance point on the branch. Then use wire to attach two cross-line swivels at this mark, one above the branch and one below it, as shown in the photo to the right. Repeat to find the balance point of the middle branch and attach two cross-line swivels to it as before. Find the balance point of the lowest branch and attach one cross-line swivel to it.

30. To assemble and hang the mobile, triple-knot a length of monofilament to the upper swivel on the branch that will be highest. Tie this monofilament onto the ceiling hook; then cut off and discard the old monofilament. To suspend the middle branch from the highest branch, triple-knot a short length of monofilament between the cross-line swivels on the branches. Be sure to adjust the relative heights of the two branches so they don't touch each other as they turn. Discard the old monofilament. Repeat to attach the third (and lowest) branch. Your mobile is ready to display!

Circle of Beads Wind Chime

Designer Jacqueline Janes fashioned her gorgeous chime with complementary black and bone-colored beads in exotic shapes and sizes. With the incredible variety of exquisite beads available these days, designing your own unique, beaded wind chime will be a snap.

Materials and Supplies

Steel wool

Nail

8" plastic or coated metal ring

3½' of ⅝"-diameter brass tubing

10 yards of leather lacing

16 yards of 1 mm waxed polyester cord

Approximately 100 beads with holes large enough for the 1 mm cord

9 donut, pendant, or other round, flat beads with center holes

Tools

High-speed hand drill

Cutting disk drill attachment

⁹⁄₆₄" drill bit

Buffing wheel or sandpaper

Instructions

1. Use the hand drill and cutting disk to cut the brass tubing into six pieces, varying in length from 5" to 7".

2. With the ⁹⁄₆₄" drill bit, bore a hole through both walls of each tube, about ½" from one end.

3. Smooth the drill holes and the ends of each tube with steel wool; then buff them with a buffing wheel or sandpaper.

4. Tightly wrap leather lacing all around the plastic or coated metal ring, leaving a few inches of lacing free before and after wrapping. Double knot both ends of the lacing and secure the knots with extra-strength craft glue. Trim off the excess lacing.

5. Cut the polyester cord into sixteen 1-yard lengths. Tie one end of each cord to the ring, spacing the lengths evenly around the entire circumference. Use a drop or two of glue to secure each knot; then trim the ends.

6. Thread beads onto the cords, fixing each bead in place with a knot above and below. Finish each cord with a donut bead, pendant bead, or length of brass tubing. Secure the last knot in each cord with a drop of glue before trimming the excess cord.

7. Cut four 12" lengths from the remaining leather lacing. Spacing them evenly, tie the lengths to the ring. Gather the lengths together and find the wind chime's point of balance

(the point where it hangs straight). Tie the loose ends of the lacing together and secure them with a drop of glue. Trim any excess lacing and display the completed chime.

Fiesta *Wind Chime*

A really good hostess knows how to bring together that eclectic mix of guests that turns an everyday event into a fabulous fiesta. That's exactly what designer Beth Palmer has done to make this flashy and festive chime. Who would have guessed that votive candleholders, ordinary hardware-store washers, and a couple of clay pots could be so much fun together?

Tools

Fine-tipped paintbrushes

Metal punch (see "Tips")

Tin snips

Needlenose pliers

Scissors

Tape measure

Tips

~If you don't own a metal punch, just use a hammer and a large nail or an awl.

~Believe it or not, any small, lightweight can—including aluminum cat-food cans—can take the place of the candleholders.

Materials and Supplies

Acrylic paints

1 clay flower pot, 4" in diameter

1 clay flower pot, 2" in diameter

Water-based urethane or acrylic sealer

12' of decorative or kite-flying cord

Several metal votive candleholders (see "Tips")

Several 6 mm beads

Several small bells

Several flat metal washers, ¾" in diameter

Threaded hook

S-hook

Chain or cord

Instructions

1. Using acrylic paints and fine-tipped brushes, paint any designs you like on the exteriors of the flower pots. Allow the paint to dry for three to five hours; then cover the exterior of each pot with a water-based sealer.

2. With a metal punch (or a hammer and nail or awl), punch a hole through the center of each metal candleholder.

3. Using tin snips, make several parallel cuts in the sides of a few of the candleholders. Then use needlenose pliers to bend and roll these cut tabs upwards.

4. Cut the decorative cord into three equal lengths. Gather the lengths together, and fold them in half.

5. About 6" down from the folded ends of the looped cords, tie a very large knot. Then, using the project photo as a guide, thread the folded ends of the cords (above the knot) through the hole in the smaller flower pot. The folded cord ends should protrude from the pot's bottom, and the knot should prevent the pot from slipping downward.

6. Tie another very large knot in the folded ends, about 2" up from the small flower pot's bottom. Then thread these ends through the hole in the larger flower pot, so the larger pot is suspended above the smaller one.

7. Cut each of the six cords dangling from beneath the flower pots to a different length. Then add the metal candleholders, beads, bells, and metal washers by stringing them onto the loose ends of the cords and tying knots directly below the objects to hold them in place. Be sure to attach an object at the very end of each cord; you don't want leftover cord ends swaying uselessly in the breeze!

8. To display this wind chime, attach a hook to a porch ceiling or rafter and suspend a length of chain or cord from it. Then slip one end of an S-hook through the end of the chain (or tie it to the cord), and slip the other end of the S-hook through the folded cords at the top of the chime.

The Destructive Side of Wind

*A*t its best, the wind is a wonderful blessing to humanity—cooling hot brows on summer days, pumping water from deep below the earth's surface, providing an inexhaustible source of energy. At its worst, however, wind is one of the most destructive natural forces known to humankind. From the biting cold of a sub-zero wind chill factor to the gigantic, menacing sweep of a hurricane, wind in one of its many forms wreaks untold damage around the world every year.

Tornadoes represent the most intensely violent winds on the planet. Meteorologists have estimated that the strongest of these storms have wind speeds of over 500 miles per hour—enough force to destroy anything in their paths. Dark, swiftly spinning funnels of clouds, tornadoes usually occur before cold fronts; however, they sometimes develop in the wake of cold fronts or in advance of warm fronts. No one knows for sure exactly how or why tornadoes form, but we do have a good idea of when and where they're likely to appear. Tornadoes are most common in the spring and summer, particularly during the afternoons; however, they've been spotted during every month of the year and at every time of the day or night. The Midwestern United States is generally recognized as the tornado capital of the world, but the United Kingdom, Italy, New Zealand, and Australia suffer their fair share, too.

Wherever a tornado touches down, it cuts a swath of acute destruction. Fortunately, this swath is usually no more than 170 feet wide and 5 to 15 miles long. A huge, swirling hurricane, on the other hand, can stretch up to 2,000 miles from one edge to the other, with winds of up to 180 miles per hour near the storm's center. These tremendous winds are at the root of a hurricane's destructive force, whipping up waves, driving powerful storm surges, felling trees, and snapping power lines.

The winds are also at the root of the storm's name. The word "hurricane" comes from a West Indian word, "huracan," which means "big wind." Hurricanes that occur in the western Pacific are called "typhoons," from the Chinese word, "taifun," meaning "great wind."

Other, smaller forces of wind can cause problems, too. Pilots, for instance, need to be well aware of wind shear, which is a sudden change in wind speed or direction. When you're flying in a plane, and you feel a turbulent bump, it's usually caused by wind shear.

Anyone who's walked outside on a windy winter morning can testify to the wind's biting effect. A wind chill factor—the combination of wind speed and air temperature—of ⁻30°F can be every bit as dangerous as an actual ⁻30°F temperature.

So, as you enjoy those fresh spring breezes and gentle summer zephyrs, keep in mind that the wind does have a less halcyon side.

Sunflower Wind Chime

What's a sunflower without a curious bee nearby? As well as being a wonderful musical ornament for your porch or garden, this project, designed by Mike Durkin, is perfect for beginning woodworkers.

Tools

Tape measure

Pencil

Compass

Jigsaw

Coping saw

Clamps

Screwdriver

Paintbrushes

Pliers

Electric drill

¹⁄₁₆", ³⁄₁₆", and ¼" drill bits

Tips

~To make the bee antennae, Mike used 1¼"-long wooden wheel axles that he found at a craft store. (The axles come with knobs on their ends.) If you have trouble finding these, just use short lengths of ³⁄₈"-diameter dowel.

~See pages 12-13 for instructios on making wind chime tubes

Materials and Supplies

Sandpaper

Wood glue

Exterior paints

6' of heavy fishing line

Cutting List

Number	Part Name	Dimensions
2	Sunflowers	see figure 1
1	Wood circle	¾" x 3" diameter
2	Bee wings	see figure 2

Lumber and Hardware

1	Pine 1 x 10, 24" long
2	Large round wooden beads, each with one flat surface
1	Piece of ⅛"-thick plywood, about 12" x 12"
2	¼"-diameter dowels, each 1" long
1	Large wooden egg
1	Round toothpick
2	³⁄₁₆"-diameter dowels, each 1¼" long (see "Tips")
2	¾" drywall screws
1	Fishing swivel, cross-line type
8	¼" screw eyes
5	Wind-chime tubes, 8", 9", 10", 11", and 12" long
1	Fishing swivel, safety-pin type
1	Metal or sturdy plastic split ring
1	½" or ¾" screw eye

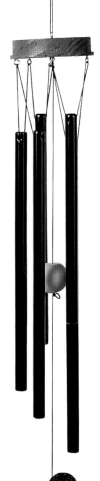

Instructions

1. Photocopy the sunflower pattern shown in figure 1, enlarging it as indicated. Also make a copy of figure 2 (the pattern for the bee wing). Set the wing pattern aside and transfer the sunflower pattern—twice—to the 1 x 10 pine. Also mark a 3"-diameter circle on the board.

2. Cut out the two sunflowers and the circle. Sand the edges of all three pieces well.

3. Glue the faces of the two sunflowers together, positioning them as shown in the project photo. Clamp them together until the glue has dried. Then paint the sunflower as desired. Also paint the 3"-diameter circle and one of the wooden beads.

4. Insert the point of a ¾" drywall screw through one end of a cross-line fishing swivel. Then turn the screw into the face of the sunflower, positioning it at either of the two screw locations shown in figure 1.

5. On one face of the 3"-diameter circle, mark the center point and insert a small screw eye at that mark.

6. Loop an 8" length of fishing line through the screw eye and through the other end of the fishing swivel. Then tie the ends of the line together.

7. Mark the center point on the bottom face of the 3"-diameter circle and insert a small screw eye at that point. Turn five screw eyes into the circle's bottom face, positioning them at equal distances and close to the circle's edge.

8. To assemble the chime, start by tying a 34" length of fishing line to one of the five screw eyes. Thread the free end of the line through the holes at the upper end of one of the wind-chime tubes. Then tie the thread to the next screw eye. Repeat to assemble all the tubes, tying the thread off again at the first screw eye.

9. Tie a 24" length of fishing line to the screw eye in the bottom center of the wooden circle.

10. Thread the painted wooden bead onto this line, positioning it about halfway down the lengths of the wind-chime tubes. To hold it in place, tie a knot in the fishing line directly beneath it. Set this assembly aside while you work on the bee.

11. Transfer the bee wing pattern (figure 2) to the plywood, twice. Cut the wings out and sand their edges.

12. To assemble the bee wings, first cut a ¼"-deep notch in one end of each 1"-long dowel (see fig. 3). Then glue a wing in place at each notch.

13. Insert a small screw eye into the top of the egg. Then drill an angled 1⁄16"-diameter hole in one end of the egg for the toothpick tail. Also drill two ¼"-diameter holes, ½" deep, for the two wing shafts. Finally, glue the wing shafts and toothpick tail into these holes.

14. In the unpainted wooden bead, drill two 3⁄16"-diameter holes, ¼" deep for the 3⁄16"-diameter wheel-axle or dowel antennae. Glue the antennae into these holes.

15. Glue the unpainted bead to the egg. When the glue has dried, paint the bee as desired. Then attach the bee to the chime by tying the fishing line to the screw eye in its top.

16. To suspend the chime, first insert the other ¾" drywall screw into the sunflower, as shown in figure 1.

Figure 1

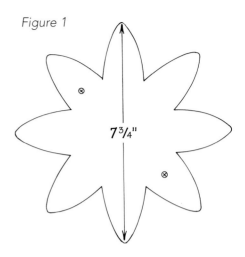

7³⁄₄"

Figure 2

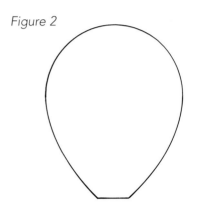

Figure 3

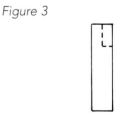

Before tightening the screw down, tie a 6" length of fishing line to it. Tie the other end of this line to the closed-loop end of a safety-pin fishing swivel and fasten the snap end to a metal or plastic ring.

17. Suspend the chime by hooking the split ring onto a ½" or ¾" screw eye or hook inserted in a ceiling or overhead beam.

Lucky Horseshoe *Wind Chime*

Since ancient times, folks in Europe have hung horseshoes over doorways and on barn sides as good luck charms. Creative seven-year-old Charlie Bennett designed this quintuple-y lucky wind chime with a little help from mom, Karen. Not only is this extra auspicious project easy to make, it's surprisingly tuneful, too.

Tools

Drill

¼" drill bit

Handsaw

Scissors

Tip

~Youthful designers should let a parent or older friend in on the fun by having them cut the tree branch.

Materials and Supplies

1 tree branch, about 1" thick and 1' long

5 horseshoes

2 leather shoelaces, 72" long

Instructions

1. Use a ¼" drill bit to bore seven holes through the branch, starting about 1" from either end and spacing the holes about 1½" apart.

2. Cut five 18" lengths from the leather shoelaces.

3. Tie a horseshoe to one end of each length of shoelace.

4. Thread the other end of each shoelace through one of the five inside holes on the branch. (The two outside holes are for the display loop.) Tie the strings in place around the branch.

5. Cut the remaining 54" piece of leather in half. Thread the doubled lengths through the outer holes in the branch and tie knots at both ends to keep them in place. (Charlie tied the knots on the underside of the branch.)

6. Display the chime any place that could use a little extra luck.

Gilded Leaves *Mobile*

Designer Genevieve Burda's simple mobile will add a touch of understated elegance to any window. With its muted gold tones, this mobile is especially lovely during the holiday season.

Tools

Wire cutters

Small kitchen sponge

Sturdy straight pins

Thimble

Materials and Supplies

Heavy-bodied, dried leaves

Two-pronged dried branch, preferably from the same kind of tree as the leaves

Newspaper

Gold liquid leafing solution (see "Tips")

Gold spray paint

Gold wire, 26- or 28-gauge

Tips

~*Genevieve used magnolia leaves on her mobile, but any heavy-bodied leaves will do.*

~*Most arts and crafts stores carry liquid leafing solution in antique gold, silver, bronze, and copper. Choose your favorite, but remember to use spray paint and wire to match.*

~*Follow the liquid leafing and spray paint manufacturer's safety instructions regarding proper ventilation.*

~*Genevieve used fine-gauge gold wire to suspend the leaves on her mobile, but lengths of thin satin ribbon in gold or red would look lovely, too, and would add an even more festive feel to a holiday window.*

Instructions

1. Select a work surface in a well-ventilated area. Cover the entire work surface with newspaper.

2. Decide how many leaves you'd like on your mobile. Genevieve suggests using an odd number such as five, seven, or nine. Lay about half the leaves on the newspaper and coat them with spray paint.

3. While the spray-painted leaves are drying, use a kitchen sponge to apply liquid leafing solution to the other leaves and the branch.

4. Apply several more layers of spray paint and liquid leafing solution, until you're satisfied with the color and texture. Be sure to allow each coat to dry before applying another.

5. Cut a length of wire about 12" long for each leaf.

6. When the leaves are completely dry, thread them onto the wires. Start by placing the stem of each leaf against a wooden block or some other solid object. Use a very sturdy straight pin to pierce a hole near the top of each leaf's stem. (Protect your finger with a thimble while you're doing this.) Thread about 1" of wire through each hole and twist it around the stem.

7. Suspend the leaves in a pleasing arrangement by twisting the loose ends of the wire along the branch.

8. Cut three 14" lengths of wire and attach one end of each wire to the branch. Twist the wires together at their tops and form them into a loop.

9. Select a window and display your mobile.

Whence Comes the Wind?

Wind, whether it's a hurricane or a gentle breeze, is nothing more than air in motion. But what makes air move to form wind? The answer, of course, is the sun.

Our sun heats up the Earth's atmosphere, but because the planet is roughly spherical and full of mountains and oceans and deserts, this heating is uneven; some places receive and absorb more of the sun's heat than others. (Think of Death Valley in California compared to Stockholm, Sweden.) It's this difference in global temperatures that causes wind.

Anyone who's ever stepped into a sweltering attic on a summer day knows that hot air rises. Hot air also expands. And that's exactly what happens with the atmosphere in those parts of the world where it's warmer than in other places—the air rises and expands; in other words, it begins to move. As the warm air rises, cooler air rushes in to take its place, and that's how wind is formed.

Shape Shifter Mobile

As it spins and twists in the wind, this intriguing mobile actually seems to change shape. From star to double diamond to endless in-between forms, designer Kevin Smith's creation will captivate all who behold its metamorphoses.

Tools

Tape measure
Hacksaw
Rasp

Materials and Supplies

10' of schedule 40 PVC pipe,
   ½" inside diameter (see "Tips")

12 90° schedule 40 PVC pipe
   elbows, ½" inside diameter

PVC solvent cement (see "Tips")

Newspaper

Acrylic spray paint

Tips

~Plumbing-supply and hardware stores sell PVC pipe in 10' lengths. Although you'll have to buy the full 10' length, some stores will cut it into the sections you need.

~Jars of PVC solvent cement come with built-in applicators, so you won't need a paintbrush.

Instructions

1. Use a hacksaw to cut 12 lengths of PVC pipe, each 6" long. Then smooth the pipe ends with a rasp.

2. Sit down on the floor with the book, the PVC pipe pieces, and the PVC elbows. Turn the book so that the display strings in the project photos all point to the right. Using as a model the photo that will now be at the upper left and starting with the V-shape at its bottom, piece the mobile together. The project is assembled correctly when you can position it so that three points touch the ground.

3. Now glue all the pieces together by removing the pipe lengths from the elbows one at a time, applying the cement to each elbow's interior, and inserting the lengths back into the elbows. Allow the cement to dry completely.

4. Spray paint the mobile outside or in a well-ventilated area, making sure to protect your work surface with several layers of newspaper. Let the paint dry and apply a second coat if necessary.

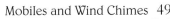

Chapter 3

Windsocks and Wind Vanes

Wouldn't it be nice to know what the weather's going to be like this afternoon—not downtown, or 20 miles to the south—but right in your own backyard? You could plan a picnic without fear of a surprise storm chasing you indoors in the middle of dessert. You could dash to the grocery store to stock up on bread and milk well before the big snowstorm hits. Most important of all, you'd know for sure if it's going to be a good day to call in sick with a malady that requires you to spend at least eight hours stretched in the chaise lounge out back, soaking up sun.

Well, believe it or not, a wind vane or windsock can be the key to your personal weather forecast—and hence, your passport to an afternoon of iced tea-sipping and sunbathing. Very often, the direction from which the wind blows can tell you all you need to know about the day's weather.

Depending on where you live, a gale from the east may precede a downpour, while a breeze from the south may herald sunny skies. Of course, winds in different places mean different things, but once you've figured out what your region's winds foretell, you'll be forecasting weather with the best of them—all with the aid of the time-honored wind vane and its close cousin, the windsock.

You certainly won't be the first person to look to one of these whimsical wind tools for weather-reading purposes. For as long as there have been farmers, sailors, picnickers, and sunbathers, people have needed some way to predict the weather. About 2,000 years ago, the Greeks invented the wind vane to do just that.

The first wind vane in recorded history depicted the Greek god of the sea, Triton. The gilded figure of the half-man, half-fish deity stood atop the Tower of the Winds in Athens in 48 B.C. In his hand, Triton held a pointed wand that indicated from which direction the wind was blowing.

Before long, other figures got into the weather forecasting business, too. As the wind vane grew in popularity and spread across Europe, animals drawn from fables quickly surpassed gods and goddesses as favorite wind-vane subjects. In the ninth century, the Pope decreed that the symbol of a rooster adorn the rooftops of all Christian

churches to warn against faltering faith. (The rooster was a symbol of Peter's betrayal of Christ.)

The rooster remained a popular subject even after the wind vane moved west to the New World; however, farmers and others who lived too far away to see a church-steeple vane or other town wind vane often fashioned their own, incorporating scenes from their everyday lives. Wind vanes featuring farm animals, human figures, and even grasshoppers crowned the roofs of all kinds of buildings, from modest homes to plantation estates.

With the onset of the Industrial Revolution, however, the wind vane's importance began to wane. Millions of people left behind farm work in the

country for factory work in the city. Although the wind vane remained an important source of information for many people, for the vast majority, it became little more than a quaint, decorative antique.

Just about the time the wind vane seemed to be on its way out, the windsock suddenly arrived on the scene—the aviation scene, that is. From the earliest days on the wind-swept dunes at Kitty Hawk, aviators recognized the importance of wind direction to flight, or more specifically, to landing. Early on, windsocks provided pilots with valuable information about wind direction and velocity. Even today, most helipads and many airports around the world still employ windsocks as standard equipment.

In the years since their first appearance on the airfields, some windsocks have changed shape, dressed up, and altogether left behind their utilitarian roots. These fanciful new windsocks are like crosses between their workhorse, runway ancestors and bright, swooping kites. Although they still indicate wind direction, they also add color and flash wherever they're displayed.

And that's just what the fun and functional windsocks and wind vanes in this chapter will do for your front porch, rooftop, or flower garden. Even if you'd rather turn on the TV for a weather report, you'll still enjoy these delightful projects.

When-Pigs-Fly *Wind Vane*

Pigs do fly, as Robin Clark clearly proves with this imaginative wind vane! The project is an easy one, so don't hesitate to try making it even if you've never worked with wood before.

Tools

Tape measure
Straightedge
Pencil
Clamps
Jigsaw or coping saw
Drill
$\frac{1}{16}$" and $\frac{3}{16}$" drill bits
Metal file
Hammer
Screwdriver
Paintbrushes

Supplies

Sandpaper
Wood glue
Exterior paint

Lumber and Hardware

1	Piece of $\frac{1}{2}$"-thick plywood or balsa, 10" x 6"
1	Piece of $\frac{1}{4}$"-thick plywood or balsa, 6" x 6"
1	Pine 1 x 4, 16" long
1	$\frac{1}{16}$"-diameter wire, 2" long
2	$1\frac{1}{4}$" brads
~	Several half-penny nails
1	$\frac{3}{16}$"-diameter metal rod, 36" to 48" long
1	Pine 1 x 8, 12" long (optional base; see step 10)
1	$2\frac{1}{2}$" 8-penny nail (optional base; see step 10)
4	No. 6 x $1\frac{1}{4}$" wood screws (optional base; see step 10)

Cutting List

Number	Part Name	Dimensions
1	Pig	See figure 1
1	Arrow	See figure 1
2	Wings	See figure 2

Tips

~ Robin Clark, who designed this wind vane, made the pig and its wings with $\frac{1}{4}$"- and $\frac{1}{2}$"-thick hardwood, but if you don't have access to hardwoods, just use $\frac{1}{4}$"- and $\frac{1}{2}$"-thick plywood or balsa instead. Balsa is available from many craft stores.

~ In steps 9 and 10, you'll find explanations of two different ways to display this project.

Instructions

1. To create cutting patterns for the pig, arrow, and wings, make enlarged photocopies of figures 1 and 2. The pig's body (fig. 1) should be 9" long from the tip of its snout to its rear; the arrow pattern should be 15¾" long; and the longest dimension of the wing pattern (fig. 2) should be 4¾".

2. Trace the pig outline onto ½"-thick plywood or balsa; the wing outline onto ¼"-thick plywood or balsa (twice, to make two wings); and the outline of the arrow onto the pine 1 x 4.

3. Before cutting out the wing shapes, clamp the ¼" plywood to your work surface and, using a jigsaw or coping saw, cut each wing's straight edge to a 45° bevel (see the dotted line in fig. 2); the wings must slant backward when they're glued to the body. Then cut out the wing shapes.

4. Cut out the pig and arrow. Smooth all the edges of the four cut shapes, except for the beveled wing edges, by sanding them well.

5. With a ¹⁄₁₆" drill bit, bore a hole in the pig (see fig. 1) for the tail.

6. To make the tail, wrap the 2" length of ¹⁄₁₆"-diameter wire around and around any tubular object (dowels or pens work well). Slip the wire off the tube; then dab one end in some glue and insert it into the hole in the pig. To secure the tail firmly, you may want to press a sliver of wood into the hole as well.

7. Glue one wing onto the pig (see fig. 1) and allow the glue to set. Then glue the other wing in place on the other side.

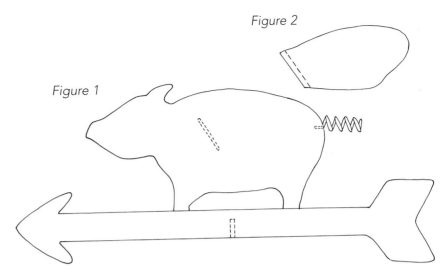

Figure 2

Figure 1

8. Glue the pig to the top edge of the arrow, centering its front foot 6" back from the arrow tip. Then drive two 1¼" brads through the bottom edge of the arrow and up into the pig's feet.

9. This wind vane can be displayed in two different ways. If you'd like to set it up on a flat surface such as a garden table or bench, skip this step and go on to step 10. To mount the project as shown in the project photo, first use a metal file to taper and narrow one end of a ³⁄₁₆"-diameter metal rod. Then find the pig's balance point by placing the bottom edge of the arrow on top of the tapered end of the upright rod and moving the arrow back and forth until the wind vane doesn't tilt forward or backward. Mark the balance point on the bottom edge of the arrow; then drill a centered ³⁄₁₆"-diameter hole, about ⅝" deep. (If you'd like to line this hole to protect it from wear and tear, refer to the Mercury Wind Vane project on pages 70-73.)

10. For table-top display, your wind vane will need a flat, relatively heavy base. First drill a ⅛"-diameter hole at the balance point on the bottom of the arrow (see step 9). Then cut two squares from the 1 x 8: a 5" x 5" square and a 6½" x 6½" square. (If you have a table saw, you may want to bevel the edges of these squares.) Drive a 2½"-long 8-penny nail through the center of the smaller square, allowing the pointed end to protrude from the square's top face. Then center the smaller square on top of the larger one and attach it by inserting four No. 6 x 1¼" wood screws from the bottom of the larger square.

11. Paint the wind vane as desired. When the paint has dried, set up the vane by fitting the hole in the arrow over the metal rod or nail.

Trumpeting Angel *Wind Vane*

This stunning steel wind vane and the variations presented with it were designed by expert metalsmith Jeffrey Hall. Although these projects aren't difficult for an experienced welder to make, they do require some familiarity with an oxy-acetylene torch. If you've never cut metal or brazed with one of these torches, indulge yourself in a good welding course, or bribe a metalsmithing friend to coach you through this project step by step. And no matter how proficient you are, be sure to read the tips on pages 10-12.

Materials

Sheet steel, 3/32" thick, approximately 12" x 12"

1 stick welder's chalk

3' of 1/4"-outer-diameter steel rod

Copper sheet, 1/32"-thick, 6" x 6"

2' of 1/8"- to 3/16"-diameter bronze brazing rod

Powder flux

Nail spike, 3/8" outer diameter, 10" to 12" long

Metal tubing, 1/2" outer diameter, 3/8" inner diameter, 4½" long

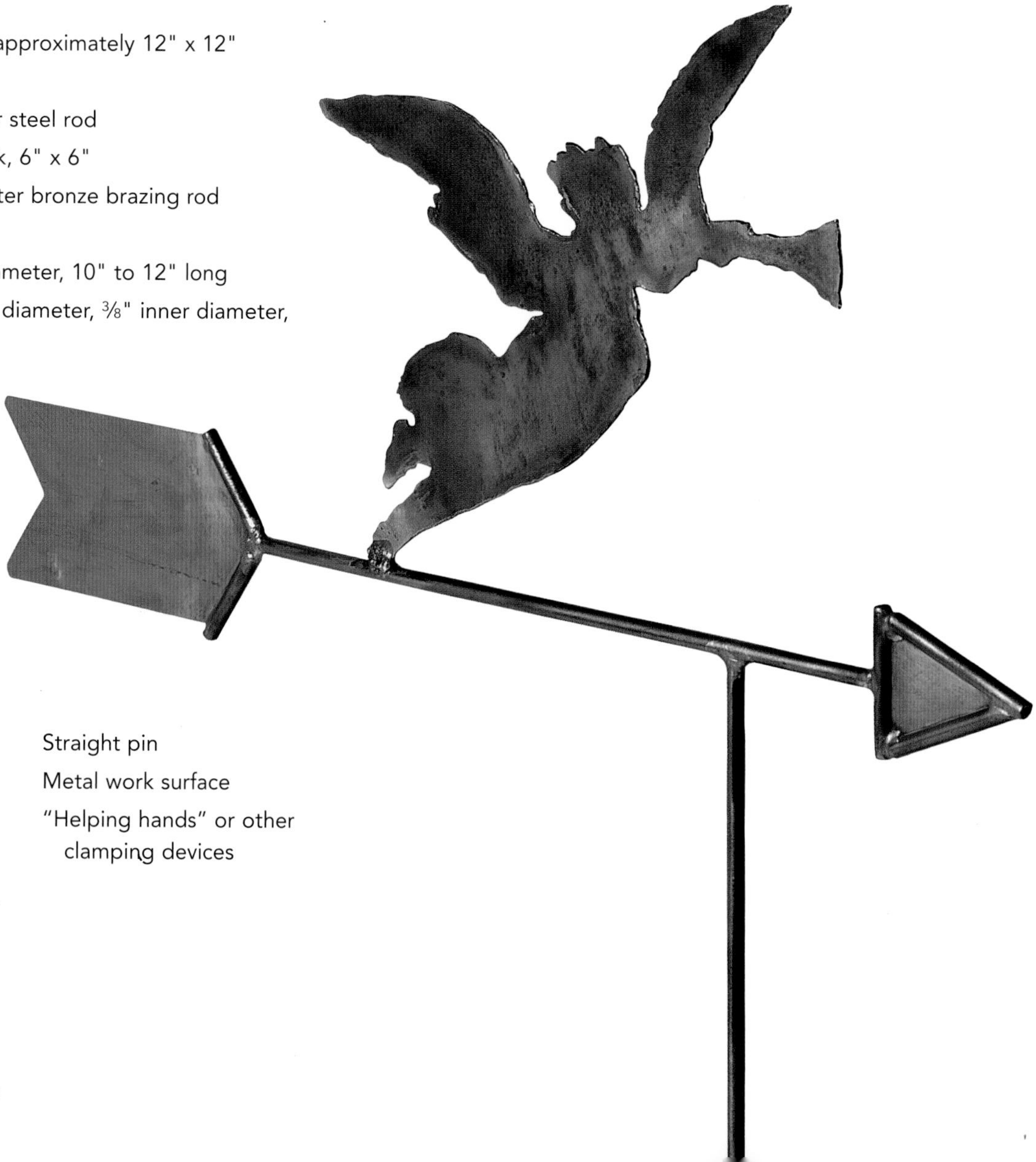

Tools

Clear goggles

#5 welder's goggles

Respirator

Heavy leather or welder's gloves

Grinding wheel

Wire brush (see "Tips")

Scissors

Tin snips

Oxy-acetylene torch

Hacksaw

Straight pin

Metal work surface

"Helping hands" or other clamping devices

Tips

~For an introduction to basic brazing techniques, see pages 10-12.

~You'll find most of the required materials at metal-supply, welding-supply, or hardware stores. Copper sheeting is also available from roofing stores, where it's sold as "copper flashing."

~If you have a bench or angle grinder with a wire wheel, use it instead of a wire brush.

~Small magnets can help hold pieces in place as you work.

~Raw steel (#1020 mild steel is the most common type) works best for this project and the variations that follow.

~Wear gloves and clear goggles whenever you're grinding or brushing the steel, and wear gloves and welder's goggles whenever you're cutting the metal or brazing it.

~Ideally, torch work should be done on a heavy metal surface.

Instructions

1. Make photocopies of the angel and arrow feather patterns shown in figures 1 and 2, enlarging them until the distance between the tips of the angel's wings is approximately 8½" and the arrow feather is about 5¼" long.

2. Clean the sheet steel thoroughly with a wire brush. (Steel that isn't clean will be difficult to cut and weld.)

3. Cut out the pattern for the angel body and use welder's chalk to trace its outline onto the sheet steel. Then use a torch to cut out the steel shape.

4. After the angel has cooled, use a grinding wheel to remove slag left from the cutting process and a wire wheel to remove any burrs. Be sure to wear gloves and clear goggles.

5. Using a hacksaw, cut the ¼"-diameter steel rod into seven pieces: one 12" long, three 2" long, two 2¾" long, and one 9" long.

6. Arrange a 2"-long steel rod and two 2¾"-long rods on top of the copper sheet to form an isosceles triangle. Then use a straight pin to scribe the interior of the triangle onto the copper. Cut out the copper arrowhead shape with tin snips.

7. Arrange the three rods and the copper to form an arrowhead. Heat the brazing rod, dip it into flux powder, and carefully braze the three corners to attach the rods to the copper. (Copper melts at around 2000°F, and steel melts at around 2900°F, so be careful not to overheat the copper.) When the arrowhead has cooled, flip it over and braze the other side in the same fashion. The brazing rod should fill in the spaces at the corners.

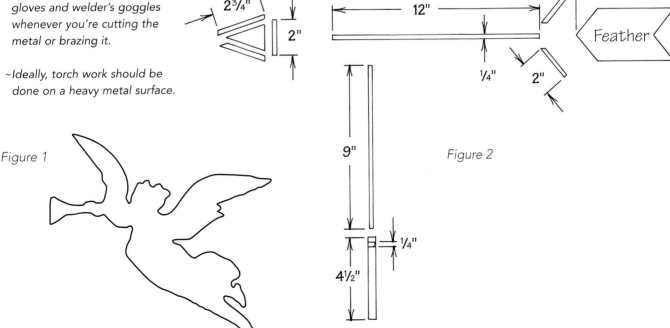

Figure 1

Figure 2

8. Scribe the pattern for the arrow feather onto the copper sheet and cut out the shape with tin snips. Arrange the copper piece, two 2"-long rods, and the 12"-long rod to form an arrow shaft with tail (see fig. 2). Braze the pieces together, first on one side, and after the metals have cooled, on the other.

9. Center the arrowhead at the front of the arrow shaft and braze the two parts together. When the metal has cooled, flip the assembly over and braze the other side.

10. Position the 9"-long steel rod on the bottom edge of the arrow shaft, at a 90° angle to the shaft and approximately 2" to 3" behind the arrowhead.

Braze the rod onto the shaft, wait for the metal to cool, turn the assembly over, and braze the other side.

11. This wind vane is mounted by slipping a hollow tube (at the bottom of the 9"-long rod) over an upright nail spike; the vane turns on the spike. Begin by using a hacksaw to remove the head of the nail spike. Next, from the same end of the spike, cut a piece about ¼"-long. Insert this ¼"-long "plug" far enough into the 4½"-long section of metal tubing to leave about ½" of the tubing empty at the top. Carefully braze the plug inside the tubing, being careful not to let the torch get too hot as you apply heat inside the end of the tube.

12. Center the end of the 9"-long rod inside the ½"-deep end of the tubing and braze it in place, filling the gap with brazing rod. (This job is easier if you position the pieces vertically.)

13. With a grinding wheel, round off the cut edge of the nail spike. Pound the spike into a fencepost or roof crown and mount the vane by slipping the tubing over the spike. To adapt the spike for mounting on other surfaces, flatten its pointed end by cutting the tip off with a hacksaw. Then braze the cut end to a small steel plate. Drill four holes in the plate and mount it by driving screws through the holes.

Variation

A variation on the Trumpeting Angel wind vane, this classic aircraft includes no copper. The instructions are abbreviated; just refer to the Trumpeting Angel instructions for more details.

Tip

~Nylon propellers and small wheel collars are available from craft and hobby shops. You'll also find wheel collars at building-supply stores.

Tools and Materials

Sheet steel, ³⁄₃₂" thick, 2' x 2'

1 stick welder's chalk

Nylon propeller, 8" long, end to end (see "Tip")

1' of ¼"-outer-diameter steel rod

2' of ⅛"- to ³⁄₁₆"-diameter bronze brazing rod

½"-diameter flat steel washer, with ¼"-diameter hole

Powder flux

Nail spike, ⅜" outer diameter, 10" to 12" long

Metal tubing, ½" outer diameter, ⅜" inner diameter, 4½" long

¼" wheel (or shaft) collar with set screw (see "Tip")

¹⁄₁₆" Allen wrench

Instructions

1. Make a photocopy of figure 3, enlarging it until the airplane body is about 15½" long, the wing is 8½" long, and the tail is 3¾" long.

2. Clean the sheet steel thoroughly. Then transfer the patterns to it. You'll need one airplane body (omit the rod protruding from the bottom), two wings, and two tails.

3. Cut out each piece with your torch, being careful not to overheat the metal when you cut out the airplane windows. When the parts have cooled, remove any burrs or slag left by the cutting process.

4. Cut two pieces of steel rod: one 10" long and one 1¼" long. The longer piece will serve as the vertical mounting rod, and the shorter one will form part of the propeller hub.

5. Set the body flat on a metal workbench. Position one wing on the body, tilting it slightly upward, and hold it in place with a "helping hands" clamp.

6. Braze the wing onto the body, turning the parts over to braze the wing's underside as well.

7. Braze a tail piece onto the same side of the airplane in the same fashion, tilting it upward as shown in the project photo. Turn the airplane over and repeat to braze the other wing and tail onto it.

8. To form the propeller hub, insert the 1¼"-diameter rod through the washer so that ⅛" of the rod extends beyond the washer face. Braze the two parts together only on the side from which the ⅛"-long rod section protrudes. The propeller must be free to turn on the other, longer end.

Figure 3

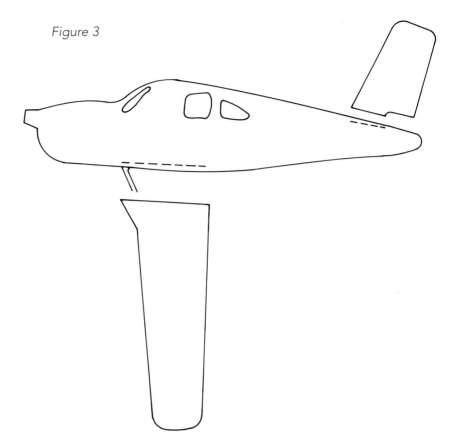

9. After the hub has cooled, carefully position the short tip of the rod on the nose of the airplane; then braze the washer and rod to the nose. The 1⅛" section of rod should extend out in front.

10. Slip the propeller onto the rod. (If the fit is too tight, enlarge the hole in the propeller with a drill and 5/16" bit.) Then slip the wheel collar onto the rod and tighten its set screw with a ¼6" Allen wrench. Make sure the propeller turns easily on the rod.

11. Braze one end of the 10"-long rod to the bottom edge of the airplane, at a distance from the propeller that is no more than one-third of the airplane's total length (see fig. 3). The vane won't turn properly if you mount the rod any farther back. If you like, you may bend the rod by hand (see the project photo).

12. To create the mounting tube and set up your wind vane, follow steps 11, 12, and 13 in the Trumpeting Angel project, brazing the 10"-long rod into the plugged tubing.

Figure 4

Variation

Ride 'em, cowboy! To make this wild-west wind vane, simply enlarge the pattern shown in figure 4 until it's approximately 9" from the horse's lowest hoof to the tip-top of the cowboy's hat. Then follow the directions for the Trumpeting Angel on pages 54-56; this project is made in exactly the same way, right down to the arrow.

Autumn Leaves *Windsock*

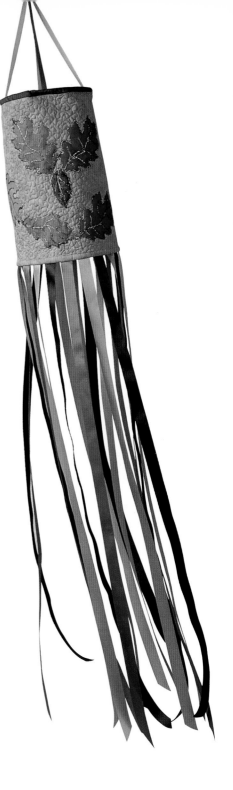

Quilter Juanita Metcalf created this gorgeous windsock in the best spirit of crisp, clear October afternoons. Autumn-colored leaves lined in gold dance across a quilted background, while satin ribbons catch the faintest fall breezes. If the weather turns less than perfect, display this project indoors where it will serve as a reminder of sunnier days.

Tools

Tape measure

Scissors

Iron

Tracing pencil

Damp washcloth

Straight pins

Sewing machine

Serger (optional)

Materials and Supplies

½ yard of cotton fabric in a neutral color for the windsock's background

1 yard of cotton or cotton-polyester fabric (¼ yard each in red, orange, brown, and yellow for the leaves)

1 yard of paper-backed fusible web

Leaves from three or four different trees

1 yard of quilt batting

18 yards of ⅞" satin ribbon (6 yards each in yellow, orange, and brown)

1 yard of muslin

3" x 24" strip of one of the leaf fabrics

1 yard of ¼" ribbon (½ yard each in yellow and orange)

Gold glitter paint

Thread to match the background fabric

7" metal ring

1" white plastic ring

Instructions

1. Cut one 13" x 23" rectangle from the background fabric and lay it right side up, with its 23" edges horizontal.

2. Cut one 9" x 9" square from each of the leaf fabrics and four 9" x 9" squares of paper-backed fusible web. Following the fusible web manufacturer's instructions, iron a square onto the wrong side of each square of leaf fabric.

3. Trace the shapes of real leaves onto the fusible web side of the leaf fabric squares. Juanita's windsock has eleven leaves, about 2" to 4" long and 1" to 3" wide.

4. Cut the leaves and remove the paper from the attached fusible web.

5. Arrange the leaves on the right side of the background fabric. With a damp washcloth, press each leaf in place.

6. Cut a 14" x 24" rectangle of batting. Lay out the batting with its 24" edges horizontal; then place the background fabric on top of the batting, leaf side up, with its 23" edges horizontal.

7. Cut the ⅞" ribbon into 18 pieces, each 1 yard long.

8. Starting ½" from one of the 13" ends, place the ribbon lengths vertically on top of the background fabric so that one end is flush with the bottom 23" edge. The ribbon will drape across the width of the fabric, with about 24" hanging over the background fabric's top edge. Space the ribbons ½" apart and pin them in place.

9. Cut a 14" x 24" piece of muslin and place it on top of the background fabric and ribbons, right side down, making sure that all of the ribbons are straight and even.

10. Sew together the batting, background fabric, ribbon, and muslin with a ¼" seam along the background fabric's bottom 23" edge.

11. Flip the muslin over the sewn edge so that the batting is sandwiched between the muslin and the background fabric. Press the background fabric, batting, and muslin into place; then trim the extra batting and muslin even with the background fabric.

12. Outline the leaves by machine quilting around them. Then meander quilt all over the background fabric.

13. Cut the bottom ends of the ribbons on a 90° slant.

14. Use the gold glitter paint to outline the leaves and their veins, and let the paint dry completely.

15. Bring the 13" edges together so that the fabrics form a column with the muslin side facing out. Use a serger or zig-zag stitch to sew together the edges with a ¼" seam.

16. Fold the 3" x 24" strip of leaf fabric in half lengthwise and press to form a crease. This strip will be the binding for the 7" metal ring that will hold the windsock's mouth open.

17. Place one of the strip's 24" raw edges against the top edge of the windsock, with the right side of the strip against the background fabric side of the windsock. Stitch together with a ¼" seam, overlapping the binding strip's ends.

18. Place the 7" metal ring inside the top of the windsock and fold the binding strip over it. Hand stitch the strip to the muslin side. The binding should completely cover the metal ring.

19. Run the two 18" lengths of ¼" ribbon through the 1" plastic ring.

20. Lightly mark four equally-spaced points on the mouth of the windsock. Sew one end of the ¼" ribbon to each point, so that the ends of the same piece of ribbon are sewn opposite each other.

21. Turn the windsock right side out, choose a spot to display it, and enjoy!

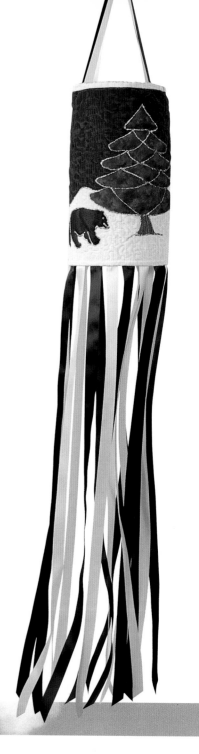

Variation

Celebrate the seasonal change from fall to winter with Juanita's lovely variation on her Autumn Leaves windsock. The whimsical Winter Scene windsock pictured above is made in almost exactly the same manner as the Autumn Leaves project; simply change the fabric colors and patterns for a whole new—slightly more chilly—look.

Gypsy Tiers *Windsock*

Vibrant. Whimsical. Romantic. If the wind were a gypsy, this is what she would wear. Fiber artist Margaret Gregg's fanciful design will make an unforgettable gift for your favorite nomadic Nor'wester.

Tools

Tape measure
Scissors
Straight pins
Sewing machine
Iron
Wire cutters
Small scissors

Materials and Supplies

2 yards of cotton fabric (¼ yard each of eight different solid colors)

Thread

1 yard of interfacing

5½ yards of 2"-wide off-white lace ribbon

⅔ yard of off-white cotton gauze

⅔ yard of muslin

12½' of 10-gauge metal wire, cut into 25", 47", 51", and 22" lengths

8' of white nylon cord, cut into four 24" lengths

Tips

~Although this isn't a project for the timid sewer, it's not as complicated as it might at first seem. Take the steps one at a time and keep in mind that the windsock is made up of four "tiers," each held open by a circle of heavy-gauge wire. Starting from the windsock's top, the first tier consists of solid vertical strips of various colored fabrics sewn together to resemble a circus tent. The second tier is an "open" arrangement of vertical, alternating lengths of lace ribbon and gauze. The third tier is a solid, narrow, horizontal "checkerboard" made from the same colors used in the first tier. The final tier consists of strips of two colors of fabric, open at the top of the tier and sewn together

towards the bottom. The instructions start at the top of the windsock and move down.

~Don't be intimidated by some of the more detailed steps, particularly those involving the construction of channels from interfacing for the circles of wire that hold open the different tiers. Margaret fashioned this windsock so that almost none of the stitching shows on its outside. Because the following directions stay true to her design, they get very detailed in some places as they explain exactly how to achieve an almost seamless-looking windsock. If visible seams don't concern you, go ahead and machine stitch the various pieces of interfacing directly to

the body of the windsock rather than worrying about the meticulous hand stitching suggested in the instructions.

Instructions

First Tier

1. Enlarge figure 1 until the pattern is 27" long from end to end.

2. Use the enlarged pattern to cut two strips from each of the eight colors of cotton fabric for a total of 16 strips.

3. Stitch the strips together one at a time with a ½" seam along their long edges, taking care to alternate the colors. Don't sew the first and last strips together yet; you'll do that in step 33. When you've finished sewing all of the strips, press the seams open and place the stitched fabric right side up on a flat surface. The narrower, curved edge of the fabric without the scalloping is the top edge of the tier, and the longer, scalloped edge is the bottom edge.

4. Cut two 1" x 24" strips of interfacing. Place the two strips across the top edge of the stitched fabric. Trim the 1" ends of the strips to match the length of the stitched fabric. Remove the interfacing.

5. Fold one strip of interfacing in half lengthwise. Center this folded piece on top of the other strip and pin it. Sew the folded piece in place, stitching very close along both edges. The bottom piece of interfacing will serve as lining, and the folded strip will serve as a channel for the wire that will hold open the first tier's top mouth.

6. Pin the sewn strips of interfacing along the top edge of the stitched fabric, with the right side (the side with the folded piece) of the interfacing against the right side of the stitched fabric. Stitch the interfacing in place with a ⅛" seam along the stitched fabric's top edge. Then fold the interfacing over the stitched fabric, wrong side to wrong side. Secure the interfacing with a few hand stitches at each of the stitched fabric's seam allowances; sewn this way, the stitching won't show on the outside of the completed windsock.

7. Now make the lining and wire channel for the bottom, scalloped edge of the stitched fabric. Cut one 2" x 50" strip and one 1" x 50" strip from the interfacing. (Alternatively, you may cut the strips in 25" lengths and sew the corresponding lengths together to form 50" strips.) Trim the short ends of the strips so that they are equal in length to the bottom edge of the stitched fabric.

8. Fold one strip of interfacing in half as before, but instead of centering it, pin the folded strip about ¼" from one edge of the second strip of interfacing. Stitch along both edges as before.

9. Pin the sewn strips of interfacing to the bottom edge of the stitched fabric, right side to right side, making sure that the folded piece is opposite the scalloped edge. Trim the interfacing to match the scallops; then sew it in place along the scallops, stitching very close to the edge. Fold the interfacing over the stitched fabric, wrong side to wrong side, and secure with hand stitches at each of the stitched fabric's seam allowances.

10. The first tier is now complete. Lay it wrong side up, with the scalloped edge horizontal.

Second Tier

11. Cut the lace ribbon into eight 23" lengths.

12. Cut eight 3½" x 23" strips from the cotton gauze.

Figure 1

13. Sew a ¼" hem along both long edges of each strip of cotton gauze; then turn each long edge in another ¼" and hem again. The strips should now be 2½" wide.

14. Pin the lengths of ribbon and gauze along the bottom, scalloped edge of the first tier, centering each length over one colored segment. Position the end of each length so that it's flush with the bottom edge of the wire channel formed by the folded strip of interfacing. Be sure to alternate lace with gauze.

15. Sew the lengths in place by hand stitching the ends to the wire channel's bottom seam allowance. This completes the second tier.

Third Tier

16. Cut eight 2⅛" x 2⅛" squares from each of the eight colors of cotton fabric. You should have 64 squares.

17. Stitch half of the squares together one at a time with a ¼" seam, being careful to alternate the colors. Stitch the remaining squares together the same way so that you have two strips of colored squares. When you've finished sewing all of the squares, press the seams open.

18. Stitch the two strips of squares together along one long edge; this gives the third tier its checkerboard effect (refer to the project photo).

19. Cut a strip of interfacing equal in width and length to the checkerboard strip, about 3¾" x 52". (As in step 7, you may also cut the interfacing into two strips and sew the ends together.)

20. Cut a second strip of interfacing 1" wide and as long as the first strip.

Fold it in half lengthwise and pin it to the first strip about ¼" from one long edge. Stitch the folded piece in place along both of its edges. The long edge with the folded strip will be the bottom of the sewn piece of interfacing.

21. Position the sewn interfacing over the checkerboard piece, right side to right side. Stitch the pieces together with a ⅛" seam along the top edge (the edge opposite the folded strip) of interfacing. Fold the interfacing over the checkerboard, wrong side to wrong side. In addition to lining the third tier and holding its circle of wire, the sewn interfacing will also join the fourth tier to the third, so leave the bottom edge (the edge with the folded piece) unsewn for now.

Fourth Tier

22. Choose two of the colored cotton fabrics that you used to make the first tier. Cut eight 2⅛" x 19½" strips from both colors.

23. Line each strip with muslin, with a ¼" seam on either long edge.

24. Remember that this tier is open at the top, but about ¾ of the way down, the strips come together to form a solid piece of fabric as shown in the project photo. Sewing only about 7" up on each strip, stitch the strips together one at a time with a ¼" seam along their long edge, taking care to alternate colors.

25. Cut two 1" strips of interfacing to match the length of the sewn strips' solid edge, about 22" to 23". (This solid edge will be the bottom edge of the fourth tier, as well as the bottom edge of the windsock.)

26. Make a channel for the tier's circle of wire following the same technique described in step 5. Sew the interfacing in place along the tier's bottom edge, stitching through the sewn strips; this seam will show on the completed windsock, so be sure to use a thread that matches one of the two colors in the tier. This completes the fourth tier.

Joining the Third Tier to the Fourth Tier

27. Lay the fourth tier piece flat, right side up, with the loose ends horizontal and pointing up.

28. Position the third tier piece (the checkerboard) on top of the fourth tier, right side to right side, with the third tier's bottom edge flush with the loose ends of the fourth tier strips. The interfacing on the third tier should be face up; fold and pin the interfacing so that it's out of the way.

29. Align the tiers so that each fourth tier strip is centered under an alternating third tier square. Remember that the third tier is 32 squares long, and the fourth tier consists of 16 strips, so there should be a strip under every other square. Pin the strips in place.

30. Stitch the fourth tier strips to the third tier squares with a ¼" seam along the top edge of the strips, being careful not to stitch through the interfacing on the third tier. (The interfacing will lay over the third and fourth tier seam, covering it.)

31. Now lay out the third and fourth tiers, wrong side up. Unpin and unfold the interfacing on the third tier and lay it back out so that it covers the tops of the fourth tier strips. Hand stitch the interfacing very close along the third tier's bottom edge, but don't stitch over the fourth tier strips.

Joining the Second Tier to the Third Tier

32. Position the first and second tiers above the third and fourth tiers, wrong side up and ribbon and gauze strips pointing down. Spacing them ½" apart, pin the gauze and lace ribbon strips along the third tier's bottom edge. Make sure that the strips fall in an even line from the first tier to the third tier. Hand stitch the strips to the third tier's interfacing along both the top and bottom edges. All of the tiers are now joined.

Completing the Windsock

33. Now form the windsock's cylindrical shape by stitching together the unsewn, vertical edges of each tier. (The second tier—the strips of lace ribbon and gauze—won't require any additional stitching.)

34. With a small pair of scissors, cut an opening no larger than ½" in each wire channel formed by the strips of folded interfacing. (There are four of these—one at both the top and bottom of the first tier, one at the bottom edge of the third tier, and one at the bottom of the fourth tier.) Be careful not to cut through any stitching. Cut three more, equally spaced openings in the wire channel at the top of the first tier—you'll use these openings to secure the nylon cord which will suspend the windsock.

35. Carefully insert the wires into the openings, shaping them into circles as you go. The 25" length goes into the first tier's top mouth, the 47" length goes into the first tier's bottom mouth, the 51" length goes into the third tier's mouth, and the 22" length goes into the fourth tier's mouth. Trim any excess wire.

36. Tie a length of nylon cord to the wire in the first tier's top mouth at each of the four openings. Gather the lengths of cord together at their loose ends and tie them together.

37. Display the windsock from a tall tree or on a large porch and watch it spin.

Butterfly *Windsock*

If a single image could sum up all the pleasures of summer, perhaps it would be the swoop of bright butterflies across a clear blue sky. Fiber artist Libby Woodruff captured the essence of summer's warm days and unexpected delights with her charming windsock, covered in fluttering butterflies.

Materials and Supplies

½ yard of ripstop nylon in light blue for the windsock body

1 yard of ripstop nylon (¼ yard each in four bright colors for butterfly wing sets and bodies)

Carbon paper

Thread

1⅛ yards of braided nylon cord

6" plastic or coated metal ring

Candle and matches

Pin clip

Fishing swivel

Tools

Tape measure

Scissors

Pencil

Tracing wheel

Straight pins

Sewing machine

Ballpoint pen

Ice pick or other metal object with a very sharp point

Tips

~This project is made with ripstop nylon so it can withstand some rain and sun. However, like any fabric, it will eventually fade and fray if you leave it out year-round or in extreme conditions.

~Remember that the ripstop nylon's dull face is its right side.

~The butterflies are the most important part of this project, so take special care when tracing, cutting, and sewing the butterfly wing sets and bodies.

~For a fun winter windsock, change the butterflies to snowflakes.

Instructions

1. Cut a 21" x 18" rectangle from the light blue ripstop nylon for the windsock's body. Then cut six 3" x 18" strips from the same fabric to make the windsock's streamers.

2. Hem ¼" around all the edges of each piece. Hem an additional ¼" along both 18" edges and one 3" edge of each streamer piece. Press all the pieces with a warm iron and set them aside.

3. Using the project photo as a guide, practice drawing butterfly wing sets and bodies on plain paper. You'll want wing sets in several shapes and sizes, with

Instructions

Body/Head and Tail

1. Cut one 18½" x 14" rectangle from the black ripstop nylon for the dragon-fly's body/head.

2. Cut one 36" x 12½" rectangle from the blue ripstop nylon for the tail.

3. For the decorative accent on the body/head, cut a 5½" x 5½" x 3½" triangle from the blue ripstop nylon.

4. Cut four 12½" x 1" strips from the black ripstop nylon for the stripes on the tail.

5. Arrange the black body/head piece with its wrong side up and its 18½" ends horizontal. Measuring down from the top, use the marking pen or tailor's chalk to mark lines across the fabric at 2", 5½", 8½", 9½", and 12½".

6. Cut five 17¾" strips of boning.

7. Position one piece of boning on the line marked at 2", centering it over the line and between the fabric's edges. Stitch it in place along both edges of the casing.

8. Center the remaining strips of bon-ing over the other marked lines and stitch in place as before.

9. Hem the fabric's upper edge; then fold it 1½" to the wrong side and stitch very close to the edge with an open zig-zag.

10. Position the blue triangle, point up, at the bottom center of the body/head piece. Stitch it into place, being careful not to stitch across the boning.

11. Arrange the tail piece right side up, with its 12½" ends horizontal. Mark a horizontal line with the mark-ing pen or tailor's chalk 10" from the bottom. With the hot knife, make ten vertical cuts up to the horizontal line, 1¼" apart. These cuts are the tail's streamers.

12. Position one 12½" x 1" black strip horizontally just above the tail streamer cuts. Stitch it into place along both edges with an open zig-zag.

13. Measuring up from the top edge of the black strip, mark horizontal lines across the fabric at 6½", 15½", and 23½." Stitch a black strip in place at each line, sewing along both edges with an open zig-zag.

14. On the body/head piece, run a gathering stitch ¼" from the lower edge. Loosen the upper thread tension by one setting and lengthen the stitch slightly; then stitch on the right side.

15. Draw up the bobbin thread and gather the piece to fit the upper edge of the tail section. Pin the body/head piece and the tail section, right sides together. Trim any excess boning; then stitch along the gathering line. Finish the seam by overcasting.

16. With the right sides together, stitch a ¼" seam along the long edges. Adjust the boning within its casing to avoid stitching over it. Overcast the seam and turn the windsock right side out.

Eyes

17. Cut two 6½" circles from the blue ripstop nylon.

18. Cut the tennis ball in half using a crafter's knife. Round objects like ten-nis balls tend to roll and slip, so be very careful during this step!

19. Wrap batting around each tennis ball half, tucking the batting's edges inside.

20. Draw a 5" circle inside each 6½" round of blue fabric. Stitch a gathering line around the marked circle on each piece. Stitch a second gathering line 1" outside the marked circles.

21. Fit one circle of fabric over the round surface of half the tennis ball by drawing up the gathering threads, inner thread first. Thread the gathering threads through a needle and take a few stitches to secure them. Repeat with the other tennis ball half.

22. Position the covered tennis ball halves on the upper edge of the wind-sock, above and to either side of the decorative blue triangle. Hand stitch the eyes in place.

Wings

23. Cut the wire into two 98" lengths and two 90" lengths. Stretch the lengths to straighten them as much as possible. The 98" lengths of wire will make wings about 36" long, and the 90" lengths of wire will make wings about 28" long.

24. Using figure 1 as a guide, bend one of the wires into the shape of a wing on the cutting mat. Allow 6" of wire to extend beyond the wing's inner edge, both top and bottom. Tape the wire in place at 12" intervals.

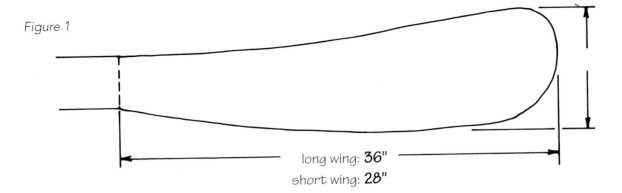

Figure 1

long wing: **36"**

short wing: **28"**

25. Double the tulle and lay it over the shaped wire. Cut the tulle around the wing shape, allowing 1" around the wire, but cutting the straight inner end of the wing flush. This will give you two pieces of wing-shaped tulle.

26. Place one piece of tulle under the shaped wire and the other on top of it. Tuck the edges of the upper piece under the wire all around the wing shape, removing and replacing the tape pieces as you go. Fold the edges of the bottom piece of tulle over the wire, keeping the fabric taut. Pin the tulle in place.

27. Install the satin stitch or open-toe embroidery foot on the sewing machine.

28. Position the wing on the machine and begin at the wing's straight inner end. Center the wire under the foot. Set the machine for zig-zag at medium length and width; then walk the hand-wheel for a few stitches to ensure that the needle won't hit the wire. Stitch the tulle in place all around, holding the fabric taut during stitching and removing the tape as you go. Trim away any excess.

29. With a medium length straight stitch, stitch the wing veins, using the project photo as a guide. Use the wire as a hoop to keep the fabric taut.

30. Make the other wings the same way, remembering to make one long and one short wing for both the right and left sides of the windsock.

31. On the windsock's body, mark the side points at each of the four lower boning strips. On each side, use a darning needle to puncture a hole just below the lower boning, just above the upper boning, and halfway between the two center boning strips. Insert the upper and lower wires of one lower (shorter) wing through the two lower holes on one side. Bend each at a right angle, toward one another, at the points where they enter the windsock. Wind the ends around each other. The lower wire of the upper wing shares a hole with the upper wire of the lower wing; its upper wire goes through the remaining hole.

Display

32. Cut three 33" lengths of cord. Fold one in half and thread both ends through a large needle. Insert the needle in the windsock, outside to inside, near the center back seam and just below the upper boning. Pull the cord halfway through, then pass the needle over the sock edge and through the loop of cord extending to the outside of the sock. Pull the cord taut. Position the other two cords near the two eyes.

33. Knot the cord ends together with an overhand knot 5" to 6" above the windsock's mouth. Knot them again 3" or 4" above the first knot. Clip off the cords ¼" above the upper knot and secure them with a generous drop of white glue.

34. Open the clip on the swivel and weave the end in and out of the cords just below the upper knot. Attach the hanging cord to the upper loop of the knot.

35. Find a nice spot and display your dragonfly!

Mercury Wind Vane

Mercury was the Roman god of commerce, theft, cunning, travel, and eloquence, but he and his Greek counterpart Hermes are best remembered as messengers of the gods. The symbolic staff (or caduceus) that Mercury held was wrapped by two entwined snakes and had two wings at its tip. In this unique wind-vane project—designed by Anders Lunde—the caduceus wings turn the staff into a propeller.

Supplies

Sandpaper
Wood glue
Exterior paints

Lumber and Hardware

1	Piece of knotty pine, ¾" x 6" x 10"
1	Piece of knotty pine, ½" x 6½" x 26" (see "Tips")
1	Piece of knotty pine, ¼" x 5½" x 8"
2	¼"-diameter dowels, each 3" long
4	⅛"-diameter dowels, each 1" long
1	1"-diameter dowel, ½" long
1	⁵⁄₁₆"-diameter dowel, 7" long
1	2"-long tension pin, ⅜" outer diameter
1	³⁄₁₆"-diameter brass tubing, ½" long (optional)
1	16-penny flathead nail
1	No. 8 brass washer
1	No. 6 x 1¼" round-head brass screw
1	¾" wire nail
1	¼"-diameter metal rod, approx. 35" long
1	20- or 30-penny nail
1	Piece of sheet aluminum, 3" x 6" (optional)

Cutting List

Number	Part Name	Dimensions
1	Head and torso	¾" x 5½" x 9"
1	Right leg	½" x 2" x 10¾"
1	Left leg	½" x 3½" x 10¼"
1	Right arm	½" x 1¼" x 8¾"
1	Left arm	½" x 2" x 9¼"
1	Right arm block	½" x 1¼" x 1½"
1	Left arm block	½" x 1¼" x 1½"
1	Right hand	½" x ¾" x 1"
4	Small wings	½" x 1" x 2½"
2	Large caduceus wings	¼" x 1½" x 3"

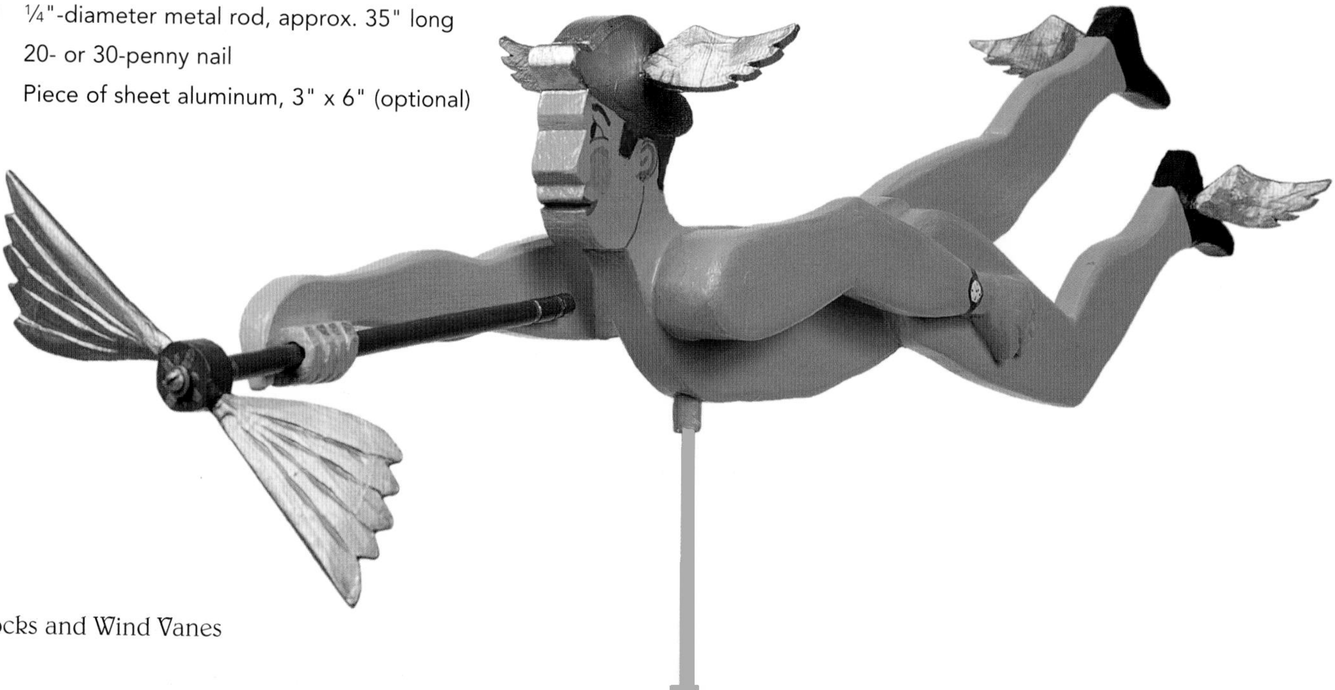

Tips

~Knotty pine doesn't come in ½" or ¼" thicknesses, so unless you own stationary power tools, you'll need to have a lumberyard cut the stock for you.

~Note that references to the "right" and "left" of this project assume that you're standing inside Mercury's body! His right arm would be your own.

~Tension pins, available at any hardware store, make great liners for the rods upon which wind vanes turn.

~When you make photocopies of figure 1, the portions you'll need as patterns will not include the staff, propeller, the wing closest to the helmet, and the wing in the foot. Just ignore these.

Tools

Tape measure

Pencil

Coping saw or band saw

C-clamps, with 3" and 4" jaw widths

Drill

$\frac{1}{32}$", $\frac{1}{16}$", $\frac{1}{8}$", $\frac{3}{16}$", $\frac{1}{4}$", $\frac{3}{8}$", and $\frac{5}{16}$" drill bits

Small carving knife

Half-round file

Screwdriver

Hammer

Paintbrushes

Hacksaw

Instructions

1. Make several photocopies of the composite figure 1, enlarging each one until the head and torso portion is 9" long from the tip of the nose to the rear. Also make two photocopies of figure 2 (the large wing), enlarging each one until it is 3½" long from stem to tip. Set the copies of figure 2 aside.

2. Transfer the pattern for the head and torso to the ¾"-thick knotty pine and use a coping saw or band saw to cut it out. Sand the exterior edges to smooth them.

3. Transfer the patterns for the two legs, two arms, and two arm blocks to the ½"-thick knotty pine. (To mark the right arm block on the stock, use as a pattern the portion of the right arm that rests behind the torso in figure 1.)

Also transfer the pattern for the right hand. Finally, transfer the small wing pattern to the stock four times.

4. Using a coping saw or band saw, carefully cut out the legs, arms, and arm blocks. (Omit the wing when cutting out the legs.) Then cut oversize blanks for the right hand piece and the four small wings; you'll carve these to shape later. Sand the arms, arm blocks, and legs well, rounding their outside edges.

5. Using figure 1 as a guide, mark the positions of the arms and legs on the head and torso piece. Then attach the legs to the head and torso piece by applying glue and clamping the pieces together with two sets of C-clamps. Attach the arm blocks to the arms in the same fashion. Also glue the right hand blank to the right arm.

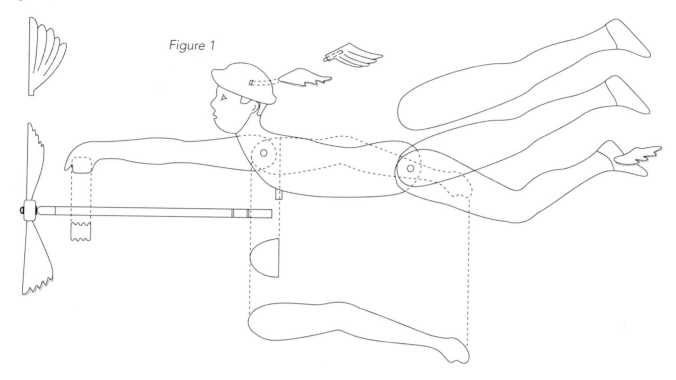

Figure 2

Figure 1

6. When the glue has dried, remove the clamps and prepare the right hand piece for the caduceus by drilling a 5/16"-diameter hole through it. Then use a carving knife and half-round file to shape the fingers. Finally, glue and clamp both arms in position on the torso (you'll need a 4"-wide C-clamp for this step).

7. To provide extra body security in the shoulder area, first drill a 1/4"-diameter hole through the shoulders, arm blocks, and torso. Insert one of the 3"-long, 1/4"-diameter dowels through the hole, applying some glue to the dowel first. Trim the ends of the dowel and sand them down to body level.

8. Repeat step 7 in the hip area, but don't drill the hole all the way through; start it on the right-leg side and stop the hole before it enters the left wrist, as the dowel shouldn't extend through the wrist of the left arm.

9. This wind vane turns on a spindle that is inserted into a lined hole in the project's bottom edge. To prepare the project for this spindle, first drill a 2"-deep hole, 3/8" in diameter, into the bottom edge of the torso (for location, see fig. 1).

10. To line the hole, you'll use a tension pin. First make a cap for the tension pin by using a hacksaw to cut off the head of a 16-penny nail. Place the nail-head cap on top of one open end of the tension pin; then insert the tension pin (cap first) into the hole you drilled in step 9.

11. Using a carving knife and half-round file, carefully carve the shapes of the four small wings, making them realistic by curving them. (Don't forget that one pair of wings will curve in one direction and the other pair will curve in the opposite direction.) As you carve, be sure to leave a stem-like

protrusion on each wing; this stem must be thick and long enough to accommodate the holes you'll drill when you take the next step.

12. In the stem of each small wing, drill a 1/8"-diameter hole, 1/2" deep. Then glue a 1" x 1/8"-diameter dowel into each hole to serve as a wing extension.

13. In the helmet and feet of the figure, drill 1/8"-diameter holes for the four small wing extensions, angling the holes slightly. Then glue the extensions into these holes to secure the wings.

14. Transfer the two large wing patterns that you made in step 1 to the 1/4"-thick knotty pine and cut out two slightly oversized blanks for these pieces. Then use your knife and file to shape the blanks into wings with feathers. Trim the wood quite thin at the feather ends, and carve a rounded extension at the stem end of each wing. Set the wings aside.

15. The ½"-long, 1"-diameter dowel will serve as a hub for the caduceus propeller. Drill two opposing ¼"-diameter holes in the hub's rim and a ³⁄₁₆"-diameter hole through its center. (You may insert a ³⁄₈"-long piece of brass tubing to serve as a liner in this hole if you like, but doing so isn't essential.) Glue the rounded extensions at the stem ends of the large wings into the holes in the hub's rim, angling them slightly as shown in the project photo. (If this is your first wind-vane project, you may want to "dry-fit" the wings first. Don't glue them in place permanently until you've taken the next step.)

16. Drill a ¹⁄₁₆"-diameter pilot hole in one end of the 7"-long, ⁵⁄₁₆"-diameter caduceus staff. Attach the hub to the staff by slipping the brass washer over the round-head brass screw, turning the

screw through the hub, slipping another brass washer over the screw threads, and turning the screw into the hole in the caduceus staff. Test the wings by blowing on them. If they're angled correctly, they should turn easily.

17. Insert the caduceus staff through the hole in the right hand piece, leaving 2" to 3" extending in front. To secure the staff, first drill a ¹⁄₃₂"-diameter pilot hole through the fingers and into the staff. Then drive a ¾" wire nail into the hole.

18. Apply two coats of exterior paint to the wind vane, letting the first coat dry thoroughly before applying the second.

19. This wind vane can be displayed in a couple of different ways. To mount it on a long steel rod, just slip one end of the rod into the lined hole in the vane's bottom edge and push the other

end of the rod into the soil. If you'd rather have Mercury spin on top of a post or porch rail, first use a hacksaw to remove the head of a 20- or 30-penny nail; then drive the nail into a post or rail, leaving at least 2¼" of the nail exposed. Next, fit the tension pin in the wind vane over the headless tip of the nail.

20. If your wind vane should refuse to turn directly into the wind, create a "rudder" for it by shaping a curved 3" x 6" piece of aluminum, painting it to resemble a cloud, and tacking it to the inside of the left leg so it hangs down below the figure.

Gods of the Wind

Throughout time and around the world, people have paid homage to the wind's power by recognizing it as a god. Hawaii's wind god was Paka; the Mayans' was Kukulcan; and the central Americans' was the plumed serpent, giver of breath, and creator god Quetzalcoatl. In Hindu mythology, the god of the winds was Vayu. The Tongans worshipped a wind god as well. His name was Laufakanaa. According to Tongan myth, the sky god sent the wind god to the Tongan island of Atat; Laufakanaa brought with him the first banana and edible roots, and he also invented the fishing net.

The Greek pantheon included many gods of the wind. Four of them—sons of Astraeos, the god of starlight and Aurora, goddess of dawn—were Zephyros (the west winds of spring), Euros (the east wind), Notos (the south wind), and Boreas (the north winter wind). Others included Apeliotes (the south-east wind); Aura (the morning wind); and Aeolus (a minor wind god and son of king Hippotes).

One wind-related myth tells the story of Zephyros' competition with his brother Boreas for the love of Chloris, goddess of flowers and buds. Much to Boreas' dismay, Chloris chose to marry Zephyros, just as all growing things prefer the warm and gentle winds of spring to the cold north winds of winter.

Even spring winds can be cruel, however. Another myth has it that Zephyros loved a youth named Hyacinthos and grew jealous when the god Apollo was also attracted to the boy. During the annual games, Zephyros took his cruel revenge. When Apollo threw his discus, Zephyros blew it in such a way that it beheaded Hyacinthos. Where the boy's blood fell, a hyacinth bloomed.

Chapter 4

Banners and Flags

Stroll through any neighborhood in your town, and you're sure to spot at least one home with a banner flying from the front-porch flagpole. Maybe it's a national flag or a pretty prefabricated pennant. Maybe it's an elaborate family coat of arms or a hand-painted welcome-home greeting. Whatever the banner, doesn't that home seem just a little brighter than all the others? A little more excited about the season, or the day, or about life in general?

Of course it does! That's because a banner is a lot more than just a swatch of cloth with a pretty design. It's really a celebration of the people living in that house. It's a statement of what's important to them, of what makes them happy, and of what they're most proud. It's a piece of themselves that they've put on display for the world. No wonder banners have become so popular in the past few years.

But don't let this recent rage for banner display fool you. Banners and flags have been around for at least as long as scribes have been recording history, and probably even longer. Ancient Egyptian art dating as far back as around 3500 B.C. depicts soldiers carrying flag-like objects into battle. Not only did the flags identify each group of combatants, but they also showed which way the wind was blowing—and thus in which direction arrows should be aimed.

The Egyptians weren't the only ancients flying banners. Persians, Greeks, and Romans all marched into battle bearing "standards"—flags created by attaching metal and fabric symbols to the tops of poles. On the other side of the world, at about the same time, the Chinese used pure silk to make what were probably the first all-cloth banners.

The banner seems to have really come into its own in Europe during the Middle Ages. That's when various ranks of the nobility began to use flags of different sizes to proclaim their status. Knights flew flags with streamers called "Schwenkels," and when the knight received a promotion, the Schwenkel would be cut from his flag. Thereafter,

the flag was known as a banner, and the knight as a "knight-banneret." Kings and queens had their own personal flags, symbolizing their authority and dominion. And who could imagine a grand medieval castle without the glorious colors of the kingdom flying from its turrets?

As the modern concept of the nation developed, so too did national flags. They first appeared in Europe and North America during the 1700s and later spread worldwide. Today, a national flag is part and parcel of being a nation. And because national flags are such potent symbols, elaborate systems for their care and display have developed over the years. For instance, a person carrying the national flag is called "the colorbearer" and must always hold the flag overhead—never horizontal; and almost all nations agree that burning is the most honorable way to dispose of a

flag that has become too tattered and worn to display.

In the United States, the Congress has actually passed a set of laws called the "flag code" to ensure that the Stars and Stripes always receives proper respect. In short, no other symbol can swell a patriot's pride like his nation's flag—just think of how you feel when you see your country's flag unfurled over an Olympic medalist.

But pride isn't the only emotion a banner can invoke. Imagine the terror sailors on the high seas must have felt when they spied a ship flying the classic grinning skull and crossed bones of the pirate's ensign. Fortunately, none of the projects in this chapter bears any resemblance to the Jolly Roger! No, the banners in the following pages are symbols of fun and happiness. They're celebrations of beauty, individuality, and good humor.

Although you won't need to follow any particular flag code for displaying your new standard, you should keep one caution in mind: Unless a banner is made of a weatherproof fabric like ripstop nylon, flag material, or heavy canvas, either display it in a protected area or bring it indoors on rainy or excessively windy days.

With that said, you'll find techniques and inspiration to make just about any kind of flag imaginable, from the delicately

dyed Sunset on Silk banner on pages 87-88 to the sturdy, weatherproof appliqué Happy Times banner on pages 89-91. Use these techniques to reproduce the featured projects or create a personalized banner all your own. Whatever you choose to do, your creation is sure to bring a new brightness, not only to your home, but to your whole neighborhood, too!

Flower Garden *Banners*

Perhaps your green thumb really isn't all that green, or maybe this year you'd like a flower garden that will come through the hottest July drought looking fresh as May. In either case, designer Ellen Zahorec's stunning paint-on-canvas banners represent the lowest-maintenance flower garden imaginable.

Materials and Supplies

~for one banner

48" x 20" piece of lightweight off-white or natural cotton canvas

Plain white paper

3 or 4 large, ½"- to 1"-thick household sponges

Textile paints in one or two shades of green and other colors of your choice

Scraps of foam core (see "Tips")

Paintbrushes of various sizes

Paper towels

Spray-on fabric weatherproofer

Tips

~See page 9 for more tips on painting fabric.

~In case you're not familiar with the term, foam core is rigid, polystyrene foam sandwiched between paper. You can find it at most craft stores.

~This banner may be weatherproofed to some extent with a fabric weatherproofing spray, but it should still come inside during downpours.

Tools

- Tape measure
- Sewing machine
- Pencil
- Scissors
- Fine-tipped felt marker
- White plate or other flat surface for use as a palette
- Hair dryer

Instructions

1. Sew a ⅛" hem along one of the fabric's 20" edges and both of its 48" edges.

2. To form the channel for a display dowel, fold the top 3" of the unhemmed edge and stitch it to the banner with a ⅛" seam. If you're using a fabric with right and wrong sides, be sure to fold and sew the edge against the wrong side.

3. Find several simple flower and leaf shapes that you like. Ellen used irises, daisies, daylilies, and forget-me-nots. Draw the shapes on plain white paper; then cut them out and trace them onto the sponges with a fine-tipped felt marker. Cut the shapes from the sponges.

4. Mix the paints as desired and spread them onto the palette in thick coats.

5. Start by painting the stems and leaves. Dip the leaf-shaped sponge in green paint and press the sponge onto the fabric, working from the bottom of the banner and moving up. (Be sure to paint only with the side of the sponge that you didn't trace on; otherwise you might end up with tracing ink on your banner.) Use the straight edges of the foam core and paintbrushes of various widths to create stems. Give the leaves and stems depth and movement by highlighting them with a second shade of green or yellow. Use paper towels to blot any excess paint from the banner.

6. Allow the stems and leaves to dry before painting the flowers. Then dip the flower-shaped sponges into the appropriate paints and press them onto the banner wherever you think flowers should appear. Accent the flowers with darker and lighter shades of the same color. Blot excess paint with a paper towel and allow the banner to dry.

7. Follow the manufacturer's instructions for heat-setting the paint.

8. Evenly coat the banner with spray-on fabric weatherproofer and allow the banner to dry according to the manufacturer's instructions.

9. Display your banner on a wooden dowel or flagpole and enjoy!

Wedding Heirloom *Banner*

Celebrate and remember the weddings in your family by creating a unique and beautiful wedding heirloom banner. The banner may be passed down from generation to generation, with each new bride adding mementos from her own wedding day. Designer Beth Smith (who now goes by the name of Beth Brock) created this lovely banner in celebration of her wedding to husband David. She anticipates the day when her daughters and nieces will add their wedding memories to the banner.

Materials and Supplies

About 2 yards of background fabric of your choice

Fabric glue

Fabric scraps and pieces of material from special occasions

Bits of ribbon and ric-rac

Other decorative accents of your choice

Thread to match the scrap fabric and material

Favors from your wedding and the weddings of friends and family

Tools

Tape measure

Scissors

Straight pins

Sewing machine

Tips

~For background material, Beth used a white polyester-cotton blend with a satiny surface and nubby texture.

~Beth decorated her banner with favors from her bridal showers and scraps of material from other special moments in her life. She included bits of satin from her senior prom dress and sprigs of tulle from her own wedding veil and the wedding headpiece of a close friend. She also used images of roses and hearts, which figured prominently in her wedding decorations. You should feel free to decorate your banner in a way that best reflects your wedding, using your own color scheme and ideas for decorations and accents.

~Small satin flowers, faux pearls, attractive buttons, gold rings, and other trinkets are widely available in most craft stores, and they make wonderful embellishments for a wedding banner.

Instructions

1. Cut two 34" x 21" rectangles and three 6" x 2½" strips from the background fabric. (You'll use the strips to make the loops for the display dowel.)

2. Cut shapes and decorative accents that you like from the scrap fabric.

3. Place one of the 34" x 21" rectangles of background fabric right side up on a flat work surface. Pin the shapes and designs on the background fabric in a pleasing arrangement.

4. Use either fabric glue or simple, neat stitches to attach the shapes and accents to the background fabric. Some materials may adhere well to the background fabric and look attractive when secured with a few drops of glue, while other fabrics may look best sewn to the banner.

5. Fold each of the three 6" x 2½" strips of background fabric in half lengthwise, with the right side of the fabric on the inside of the fold. Stitch a ½" seam all along the raw edges, leaving a 1" opening near one of the short ends. Turn the strips so that the fabric's right side is facing out. Press the strips with a warm iron.

6. Fold each strip in half to form a loop. Starting ½" from one end of the top 21" edge, place the folded strips vertically on top of the decorated rectangle of background fabric. The loops should be equally spaced, and the unfolded ends should be flush with the background fabric's edge; the folded ends should be lying against the background fabric's decorated (or right) side, pointing toward the bottom 21" edge of the rectangle. Pin the loops in place.

7. Place the other rectangle of background fabric on top of the decorated rectangle, right sides together and corners square. Stitch the rectangles and loops into place with a ½" seam, leaving a 6" opening. Backstitch on either side of the opening.

8. Turn the banner right side out and neatly stitch the opening closed.

9. Display the banner on a dowel up to 1½" in diameter.

More Special Occasion Banners

 wedding is just one of many events that a special, handmade banner can commemorate. Following are a few more ideas you might like to try:

Birthday banner
As we get older, many of us tend to lose our enthusiasm about birthdays. Learn to welcome the anniversary of your birth by creating a special banner. Every year, add something to symbolize the milestones of the year gone by and something else to represent your hopes for the year to come. Children, of course, don't need any help fostering birthday enthusiasm, but making a birthday banner will still be a lot of fun for them. Plus, it will act as an unusual scrapbook of your son or daughter's early years.

Graduation Banner
Passing notes during history class; screaming yourself hoarse at the homecoming game, then dancing with that guy you'd had a crush on for the past two months at the after-game dance; skipping physical education to get out of playing kick ball—during the month or two before graduation, you suddenly realize that you had some pretty darn good times in high school, after all. Why not get together with your friends to make a banner that will immortalize all those great memories?

Family Reunion Banner
Even if it is best that you only see Aunt Mary and Uncle Bob once a year at the annual family reunion, wouldn't it be fun to have a great big family banner to which everyone added each year?

Jig Time Bird *Flag*

Artist Jean Penland's fanciful flag features a very happy bird that kicks up its heels and flaps its wings at the slightest breeze. Fun to make and even more fun to watch, this flag requires no sewing— just a pair of scissors and a little skill with a painter's palette.

Tools

Scissors or electric hot knife

White plate or other flat surface for use as a palette

Artist's flat paintbrushes in at least three sizes

Pencil

Materials and Supplies

2 yards of white ripstop nylon

Newspaper

Acrylic paints in your choice of colors

Crafter's squeeze bottle acrylics in your choice of colors

Fast-drying enamel or acrylic spray paint in white

½"-diameter wooden dowel, 35" long

Heavy masking tape or glue

2 small screw eyes

4½' to 5' of nylon cord

Tips

~The key to this banner's no-sew construction is cutting the ripstop nylon on the bias to prevent it from fraying. If it looks as if the fabric will fray anyway, you may want to hem the cut edges.

~Remember that ripstop nylon's "dull" side is its right side.

~Paint can and does bleed through ripstop nylon; be sure to protect your work surface with several layers of newspaper.

Instructions

1. Cutting on the bias, cut a 31" x 47" rectangle from the ripstop nylon.

2. Cover a large, flat work surface (Jean recommends the floor) with several layers of newspaper.

3. You may want to sketch your design on paper before you begin painting on the ripstop nylon. If you want to reproduce Jean's happy bird, use the project photos and figure 1 as guides.

4. When you're ready to begin painting, position the rectangle of ripstop nylon on the work surface, with its right side up and short ends horizontal. Paint the flag's central character first; this is the bird in Jean's flag. If you're reproducing Jean's bird, spread a thick coat of red paint on your palette and paint the bird's body first.

5. Use crafter's squeeze bottle acrylics to draw special features on the flag's central character. Jean used the squeeze bottle acrylics in orange and yellow to outline her happy bird's legs and beak. She drew the bird's eye with green.

6. Allow the paint to dry. Then fill in the outlines with the colors of your choice. Jean mixed a little regular yellow acrylic with a few drops of orange squeeze bottle acrylic and some water to produce a great color for her bird's legs and beak. She dabbed white acrylic in the eye outline and allowed it to dry before painting the eye's iris and pupil with two shades of blue acrylic.

7. Paint the rest of the flag around the central character. Jean mixed blue acrylic with water to produce the light-textured blue shown in the project photos. She mixed yellow acrylic with a few drops of orange squeeze bottle acrylic and some water to get the yellow background.

8. Allow the paint to dry before adding additional decorative touches. Jean used short strokes with various sizes of flat-bottomed artist's paintbrushes to produce the rectangles of color on the yellow background.

9. Let the paint dry completely. Then turn the flag over. If the paint has bled through the fabric, spray the back of the flag with a fine coat of fast-drying white enamel or white acrylic paint.

10. After the spray paint has dried, turn the flag back over and lightly mark the vertical lines along which you'll make cuts. Locate the cuts where they'll create movement in the central character; Jean made five cuts: one across the bird's foot, one above its knee, and three through the flag's yellow background.

11. Turn the flag back over and center the wooden dowel 2" from the top. Fold the top of the flag over the dowel, wrong side to wrong side, and use heavy masking tape to secure the dowel firmly in place. Alternatively, fold the top edge of the flag over and stich it in place to form a channel for the dowel.

12. You may either display the flag on a dowel flagpole as shown in the photo on the opposite page or hang it from nylon cord by inserting a small screw eye into each end of the dowel and tying the cord to the screw eyes.

Figure 1

Swirling Colors *Banner*

In case you hadn't heard, marbles are back in a big way! Eleven-year-old designer Rachael Bennett brought the marble fad to fabric with this fun and fantastically colorful banner, perfect for celebrating a sunny spring day.

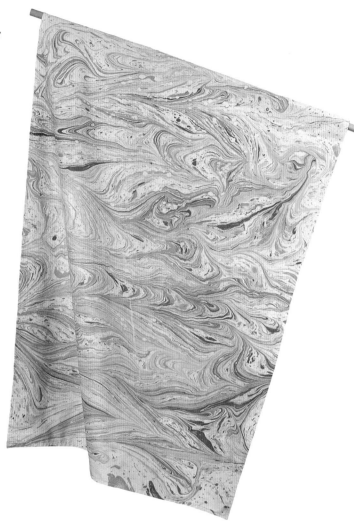

Tips

~If you can't find a plastic tub as large as the one recommended in the "Tools" list, make your own marbling tray with 1 x 4 lumber cut to the appropriate lengths and held together with angle brackets or nails. Line the bottom of the tray with a double layer of 6 ml plastic sheeting, tucked down in the corners.

~Rachael and her mom both strongly suggest that you wear old clothes while making this project!

~See pages 9-10 for more information on fabric marbling.

Materials and Supplies

2 yards of white 100% cotton fabric

Newspaper

Alum (aluminum sulfate crystals)

Methyl cellulose

Ammonia

Vinegar

Distilled water

Acrylic fabric paints in the colors of
   your choice

Tools

Scissors

Rubber gloves

Bucket

Clothespins

Plastic tub, 4' x 4' (see
   "Tips")

Wooden spoon

Measuring spoons and
   cups

Variety of paintbrushes

Comb, hair pick, or chopsticks

Handheld showerhead or garden
   hose

Iron

Tape measure

Sewing machine

Instructions

Preparing the Fabric

1. Start by washing the cotton fabric to remove any sizing. (Sizing is a stiffening agent used on many types of fabric.) Machine dry; then cut the fabric into two equal rectangles.

2. Line your entire work area with several layers of newspaper.

3. Put on rubber gloves and in a large bucket, mix a solution of ⅓ cup alum to 1 gallon of cool water. You'll want enough solution to completely submerge the rectangles of fabric. Let the fabric soak for 30 minutes; then remove and dry it on a clothesline or drying rack. Remember to wear the gloves the entire time that you're working with the alum solution.

Making the Bath

4. Pour enough distilled water into the tub to cover the bottom by 2" to 3", keeping track of how many gallons you add. Put on rubber gloves and add 4 tablespoons of methyl cellulose for every gallon of water in the tub. Using a wooden spoon, stir the solution until it's lump-free.

5. Add 2 tablespoons of ammonia for every gallon of water and stir until the mixture has thickened to the consistency of egg white. Let the mixture stand for half an hour.

6. Add 2 teaspoons of white vinegar for every gallon of water. Stir well; then let the mixture stand for 12 hours.

Marbling the Fabric

7. If you're using powdered paints, mix them according to the manufacturer's instructions. If you're using liquid paints, thin them with water until they're the consistency of light cream. You'll need about 4 to 6 fluid ounces of mixed paint for a banner the size of Rachael's.

8. Sprinkle the paints into the bath. Paintbrushes of various sizes make good sprinkling tools; dip the brush in the paint, hold it over the water with one hand, and hit the brush with the other hand to make the paint splatter onto the water. The paint should float on the water; if it sinks, add a little more water to your paint mixtures.

9. Using a comb, hair pick, or chopstick, swirl the paint into patterns, or leave the paint droplets alone for a rounded, stone effect. Experiment with the paints to get different designs.

10. Have someone help you fold one rectangle of fabric in half and gently lay it, center first, in the bath; then carefully unfold the outer edges so that the fabric lies flat in the water on top of the paint design. Leave the fabric in the bath for about 20 seconds.

11. Pick the fabric up by the edges of one short end. Let it drip over the bath for 20 to 30 seconds; then take it to the bathroom or to an outside hose—be quick! Don't let anything touch the fabric during your dash, or the paint will smear. Rinse the fabric with a handheld showerhead or a garden hose. Hang the fabric to dry.

12. Repeat the process with the second piece of fabric, adding fresh paint to the water if needed.

13. Let both rectangles of fabric dry completely; then iron them to set the paint.

Sewing the Banner

14. Measure 3" down from one short end of each rectangle of fabric; this will be the top end of the banner. Sew a ¼" hem along the edges from the top of the banner down to the 3" mark. This hem will save you the trouble of attempting to hem the sides of the channel for a display dowel once you've sewn the banner together.

15. Stitch the two pieces of fabric together—right side (painted side) to right side and corners square—with a ½" seam. Leave an opening at the bottom of the banner to turn the fabric right side out. Be sure not to stitch over the area you hemmed in step 14; this will be the channel for a display dowel.

16. Turn the banner right side out. Measure 3" down from the banner's top edge and sew the fabric together from edge to edge to create the channel for a display dowel.

17. Stitch together the opening at the bottom of the banner. Top stitch the three remaining edges of the banner, about ¼" from the edge of the fabric.

18. Display your new banner on a wooden dowel or a flagpole.

Oktoberfest Batik *Banners*

Batik artist George Summers, Jr., created these gorgeous banners as part of a set of twelve to be displayed at an Oktoberfest benefit dance. With these festive, frolicsome swaths of color flying overhead, who wouldn't want to get up and dance under the harvest moon?

Tools

Sewing machine

Frame for stretching fabric (see "Tips")

Push pins

4 tin cans of equal size

Soft lead pencil

Electric deep fryer with accurate
   temperature control

Assortment of stiff-bristled paintbrushes

Tjanting tools

Rubber gloves

2 or 3 plastic tubs to use as dye baths
   (see "Tips")

Drying rack or clothesline

Iron

Materials and Supplies

Newspaper

Medium-weight, even-grained, white, 100%
   cotton fabric (see "Tips")

Beeswax, microcrystalline wax, or commercial batik wax (see "Tips")

Cold water fiber-reactive dyes in the colors
   of your choice (see "Tips")

Plain newsprint (see "Tips")

Tips

~For instructions on making a frame for stretching fabric, see page 9.

~To get the best effect from dye baths, use a tub or some other plastic container large enough to keep the material more or less flat when it's immersed; otherwise the wax might crack, which would allow dye to go where it's not intended. George's banners are fairly large— 2¾' x 4½'—and he used a dye bath almost as large to make them. You may want to start with a smaller banner (and thus smaller tubs for dye baths) until you're ready to invest in large-scale equipment. For instance, a 1' x 2' banner would be a nice size to start with.

~To replicate George's banners, you'll need fiber-reactive dyes in yellow, red, green, purple, and turquoise.

~Mixing requirements for fiber-reactive dyes vary from brand to brand, so be sure to follow the manufacturer's directions as you blend colors and make dye baths.

~Be sure to protect your hands by wearing rubber gloves during the entire dyeing process.

~You'll use plain newsprint for lifting the wax off the banner, as explained in the directions on page 10. Don't confuse plain newsprint with newspaper; they're not the same! You can find plain newsprint in most craft stores.

~Although the following instructions give the sequence of dyeing and painting steps that George used to make his stunning banners, batik lends itself to the creativity and individuality inherent in every artist. In other words—don't feel bound to replicate the banners shown here; instead, use these projects and their instructions as an inspiration and a guide to inventing a design that's uniquely your own.

~George recommends using pure beeswax.

~See page 10 for more information about batik.

Instructions

1. Start by washing the cotton fabric to remove any sizing. (Sizing is a stiffening agent used on many types of fabric.) Machine dry the fabric.

2. Cut a rectangle the desired size of the banner from the fabric; then turn the rectangle's long edges in ¼". Turn the edges in again by the same amount and machine hem them in place.

3. Stitch a ⅛" hem along one short edge of the rectangle. This edge will be the top of the banner. (The bottom edge isn't hemmed.)

4. Fold the top edge of the banner over 1½" and stitch it in place to form the channel for a display dowel.

5. Arrange the banner on a large, flat work surface, with the short ends horizontal. Using a soft lead pencil, draw the complete design for the banner

right on the fabric. The pencil marks need to be fairly heavy to prevent them from washing off during the dye baths.

6. Protect your entire work area with several layers of newspaper, remembering to place some under your clothesline or drying rack, too.

7. Place a tin can under each corner of the frame; then stretch the fabric by securing its edges directly to the frame with push pins (as George does), or follow the directions for stretching fabric in steps 3 and 4 on page 88.

8. Prepare the first dye bath according to the dye manufacturer's instructions. (George started with a yellow dye bath for the magenta banner and a green dye bath for the turquoise banner.) Remember that the dye bath must be cold.

9. Following the directions on page 10, melt the wax in an electric deep fryer.

10. If you're making a banner similar to those shown in the project photos, start by using a tjanting tool to outline the leaves with wax; then use a stiff-bristled paintbrush to apply wax inside the blocks that will remain white, being careful to avoid getting wax inside the leaf outlines.

11. Allow the wax to dry completely; then don a pair of rubber gloves and immerse the banner in the first dye bath. Allow the fabric to soak according to the manufacturer's instructions. Remove the banner from the bath and hang it up to dry. It should be bone dry before moving on to the next step.

12. Stretch the banner in the frame again. Coat all the parts of the design that you want to remain the color of the first dye bath with wax. For instance, if you're making one of George's banners, outline leaf veins with wax using the tjanting tool. At this point, George used a paintbrush to dye the leaves their various colors. Simply daub the dye inside the wax outlines of the leaves. For the magenta banner, George covered the stars with a coat of wax at this point, too.

13. Allow the dye to dry completely; then coat the painted leaf areas with wax and let the wax dry.

14. Prepare the second dye bath (George used a red bath for the magenta banner and a turquoise bath for the turquoise banner.) Put your rubber gloves back on and immerse the banner. Remove, hang, and dry.

15. Stretch the banner on the frame again. Cover all the areas of the banner that are to remain their current color with wax. For instance, to make George's banner, use the tjanting to outline the dancing figures with wax. To make the turquoise banner, you'll also outline the stars at this point. Cover all the remaining areas with wax and allow it to dry.

16. Prepare the final dye bath. George used a deep purple as the final bath for both of his banners. Hands protected with rubber gloves, immerse the banner one last time. Dry as before.

17. When the banner is totally dry, remove the wax, following the directions on page 10.

18. Display and enjoy.

Vexillology: the Scientific Study of Flags

What does it mean to "grab the halyard" and "reeve the jack"? If someone asked, could you describe the badge on the fly, the union in the canton, the fimbration on the bunting? Are we speaking the same language here? We are if you're a vexillologist!

This funny—and most likely unfamiliar—word describes a person who explores the history, terminology, and symbolism of flags from around the world. Folks have been studying vexillology since at least as early as the mid-fourteenth century. That's when an anonymous, Spanish Franciscan monk produced the earliest and most significant work in the vexillological canon: the *Book of the Knowledge of All the Kingdoms, Lands, and Lordships That are in the World* .

Today, national and regional vexillological organizations convene to discuss their research at the bi-annual International Congress of Vexillology, founded in 1965. Congresses are held all over the globe, from Vienna, Austria to Cape Town, South Africa. True to the cause, a special flag is designed as a symbol for each congress, either by a member of the hosting organization, or by one of a number of recognized vexillologists around the world.

Sunset on Silk *Banner*

Artist Betty Kershner painted this stunning silk banner using a French dyeing technique known as serti, or fencing. In the serti technique, the artist draws a design directly on the fabric with a resist (in this case, gutta); then she applies dye to each fenced area of the design with a brush. The dye spreads right up to the resist, but not beyond; this damming effect gives the artist exacting control over design and color.

Materials and Supplies

1 yard of undyed silk

Thread

Gutta fabric resist

Cold water fiber-reactive dyes, or other fabric dyes (not paints) in yellow, fuchsia, turquoise, and black

Salt

Tools

Scissors

Frame for stretching fabric (see "Tips")

4 tin cans of equal size

Non-permanent pen

1 small squeeze bottle with fine applicator tip

Metal applicator tip for the small squeeze bottle

Small cups to hold the mixed dyes

1" foam paintbrushes, 1 for each color of dye used

Eyedropper

Sewing machine

Tips

~To paint silk with dyes, you'll need to stretch the fabric on a frame. You'll find instructions for making a simple frame on page 9.

~Many craft stores carry applicator bottles and metal tips made especially for gutta.

~Cold water fiber-reactive dyes are the best choice for this project. Some craft stores carry these dyes, but if yours doesn't, check the Internet or your library for mail-order suppliers. Fiber-reactive dyes are available premixed or in powder form; Betty uses the powdered dyes and mixes all her colors from the four listed in the "Materials and Supplies" list.

~Silk is a delicate fabric, so display this banner outside only in good weather or for special occasions. Display it inside by a breezy window the rest of the time.

Instructions

1. Cut a 31" x 35" rectangle from the silk.

2. Layer your entire work area with sheets of newspaper. Set up the frame in the work area by propping tin cans under each corner. (The cans will keep the fabric from touching the work surface.)

3. To stretch the silk on the frame, start by placing the fabric, right side up, inside the frame.

4. Thread a needle with a doubled length of thread. Make a single stitch at one corner of the fabric, running the needle back through the thread's loop to secure the stitch. Pull the thread tight. Then cut the thread, remove the needle, and tie the loose thread ends to the corresponding corner of the frame. Secure the other corners of the fabric and at least one point between each corner in the same manner, pulling the thread tight so that the fabric is stretched taut between the frame. The fabric should be suspended, with no part touching the frame or the work surface.

5. Using the project photo on the previous page as a guide, lightly draw several mountain ranges (or the design of your choice) directly on the fabric with a non-permanent pen. Be sure that each shape in the design is completely enclosed; otherwise, when you apply the dye, it will run from one area of the design to another.

6. Fill a small squeeze bottle with gutta. Fit the bottle with a metal applicator tip. Then, holding the bottle vertically with the metal tip pressed firmly against the fabric, apply gutta along the lines of your design. Again, be sure that you fully enclose (or fence off) each separate part of the design. Allow the gutta to dry completely.

7. Mix the dyes according the manufacturer's instructions, placing each color in a separate cup or small container. You'll want to experiment with the dyes to create colors you like.

8. To create the sunset effect on the fabric above the mountains, Betty dabbed horizontal bands of various colors on the fabric with 1" foam paintbrushes. She started with darker blue and grey dye at the top of the banner and gradually switched to pinks and yellows as she neared the mountains. She left some areas unpainted to allow for a gentle blending from one band of color to the next.

9. Before the dye begins to dry, use an eyedropper to drop water along the bands of color. Use a clean foam paintbrush to gently spread the water throughout the bands of dye. The water will dilute the dyes slightly and make them run into one another; use a foam paintbrush to direct the blending of colors.

10. Sprinkle a little salt over the damp fabric wherever you want a spotting effect. Each grain of salt will leave a spot on the dye.

11. Paint the mountains the same way, using the colors of your choice. You don't need to apply dye right against the lines formed by the gutta; the dye will run up to them on its own.

12. Allow the banner to dry completely; then set the colors by pressing the banner with a warm iron.

13. Rinse the banner in hot water. Let it dry; then have it professionally dry-cleaned to remove the gutta.

14. Machine hem all around the banner's edges with a ⅛" seam.

15. Fold the banner's top edge down 1½", wrong side to wrong side. (The side you painted is the right side.) Stitch along the fold's bottom edge to form the channel for a display dowel.

Wind Around the World

Bulgarian ~ viatyr	Japanese ~ kaze
Danish ~ vind	Maori (New Zealand) ~ hau, matangi
Dutch ~ spoelen, winden	
Estonian ~ tuul (or puhkpillid)	Portuguese ~ vento, sopro
French ~ vent	Rotuman (Fiji) ~ lagi
Gaelic ~ (Ireland) gaoth	Serbian ~ vetar
German ~ der Wind	Spanish ~ viento
Hungarian ~ szél	Swahili ~ homu
Indonesian ~ angin	Swedish ~ vind
Italian ~ vento	Turkish ~ ruzgar

Happy Times Appliqué *Flag*

Do these guys look fun or what? Expert sewer Rebecca Bennett, age eight, fashioned this smiling bunch with a little help from her big sister, Emily, age thirteen. Together, they created a fun appliqué flag.

Tools

Gridded cutting mat

Rotary cutter

Straight pins

Sewing machine

Satin stitch or open-toe
embroidery foot

Appliqué (or rug)
scissors

Tip

~Because this banner is made from flag material, which is pretty sturdy stuff, it can weather most seasons without damage. Most fabric stores carry flag material or will be happy to order it for you if they don't have any in stock.

Materials and Supplies

2 yards of blue flag material

⅝ yard of green flag material

⅜ yard of tan flag material

⅜ yard of gold flag material

⅜ yard of grey flag material

¼ yard each of yellow, orange, pink, and dark brown flag material

Marking pen or tailor's chalk

3 spools of black thread

Blue thread

Fabric glue

Instructions

1. Cut a 35½" x 45" rectangle from the blue flag material. Lay the rectangle, right side up, on a flat work surface, with the 35½" edges horizontal.

2. Using figure 1 (see page 91) as a guide, draw patterns for each piece on the correct color of flag material. Cut out the pieces.

3. Piece the sun in place on the rectangle of blue material, with its upper edge 6" down from the rectangle's top edge and its left edge ¼" in from the rectangle's left edge. Pin the pieces in place.

4. Pin the other pieces in place, moving from the top of the flag down. (Don't forget to pin on the giraffe's spots!) The green ground should overlap the elephant and giraffe neck pieces by about ¼", but be careful not to pin the ground over the circle that will be the lion's head and mane.

as a guide. Cut as close to the stitches as possible. Then cut the green material away from the inside of the round flowers and the tan material away from the inside of the giraffe's dark brown spots.

11. Using a regular open zig-zag and blue thread, sew a ¼" hem all around the banner.

12. Fold the top 3" of the flag over, wrong side to wrong side. (The wrong side is the side from which you cut the blue material after stitching.) Stitch the fold in place along its bottom edge to form the channel for a display dowel.

13. Finally, make cuts all along the outside circle of the lion's head to form his mane.

14. To prevent the mane from falling into the lion's face, use a little fabric glue to secure its top pieces to the banner. Leave the other mane pieces free to flutter in the wind.

5. Use a marking pen or tailor's chalk to draw the animals' eyes and smiles, as well as the butterfly's antennae.

6. On the circle that will be the lion's head and mane, measure 3" in from the outside and draw a circle; you'll stitch along this inside circle to secure the lion in place while leaving his mane free.

7. Install the satin stitch or open-toe embroidery foot on the sewing machine, adjust the zig-zag to ⅛", and thread the machine with black on both the top and bottom.

8. Stitch all the pieces into place, being careful to stitch only the marked, inner circle on the lion's head. Remember to stitch the ground piece underneath the lion's mane, rather than on top of it.

9. After you've stitched all the pieces in place, go back and stitch the animals' eyes and smiles, and the butterfly's antennae.

10. Turn the flag over, right side down. Working with the appliqué (or rug) scissors, carefully cut the blue flag material away from the interior of the stitched pieces, using the stitching

Figure 1

Chapter 5

Whirligigs and Wind Toys

Wrap a child's fingers around the staff of a flashy dime-store pinwheel and you'll soon see the effect that wind toys and whirligigs have on people of all ages: eyes light up, grins widen into big smiles, smiles turn to outright laughter.

There's just something about whirling wind toys that everyone loves. Maybe it's because people are naturally drawn to their spin and motion, or maybe it's the obvious ingenuity that goes into whirligig design. Then again, maybe it's simply because the whirligig's sole purpose *is* to delight and amuse the beholder. From the simplest pinwheel to the most elaborate mechanical gadget, these toys are meant to be nothing but fun.

And of course, people have been interested in having fun for a long time. No one knows for sure, but many believe that Europeans may have started or adopted the whirligig tradition sometime after the twelfth century. That's when the windmill made its way to Europe from the East—and there's no mistaking the resemblance between a pinwheel and its giant utilitarian cousin! Almost without a doubt, the windmill served as inspiration for the earliest whirligig artists.

Another wind-driven relative—the sailboat—carried the whirligig across the Atlantic and to the fledgling United States of America. There, the whirligig found its most enthusiastic audience yet. By the early nineteenth century whirligigs had become so ingrained in American culture that one made a cameo appearance in that most American of ghost stories, Washington Irving's "The Legend of Sleep Hollow," published in 1819.

The whirligig didn't just appear in spooky stories, either. Some were scary in their own right. One of the most popular whirligig designs—dating from about 50 years after poor Icabod Crane lost his head in Sleepy Hollow—features a creepy witch astride a whirling broomstick.

Obviously, whirligig artists have never lacked creativity, but the American craftspeople of the 1930s surpassed even their imaginative predecessors. While the Great Depression saw a decline in almost every other activity, the art of the whirligig prospered as never before.

With jobs scarce, people sought ways to busy their idle hands and minds, and designing clever spinning toys provided the perfect means.

Maybe it was the frustration of joblessness, or maybe it was the need to create something that would bring a smile to folks who didn't have much else to smile about; whatever the reason, artists of the Great Depression era took the whirligig to new heights. Designs grew to become feats of engineering, with some whirligigs featuring three or four levels of activity—all driven by a single propeller. The subject matter of whirligigs expanded, too, with many artists using their medium for wry political commentary.

Today, hobbyists all over the world are still inventing new designs and improving on old ones. Aspiring whirligig artists might find the sheer variety of designs somewhat intimidating. Not to worry, though—even in the free-wheeling world of the whirligig, some structure does exist. Anders Lunde, a renowned whirligig artist and author of several books on the subject has identified four major types of whirligigs:

wind-vane whirligigs, winged whirligigs, arm-waving whirligigs, and mechanical whirligigs.

The first type, the wind-vane whirligig, is something of an oxymoron. In the strictest sense, a whirligig's only function is to amuse and delight. A wind vane, on the other hand, serves to show the direction of the wind, and is therefore a utilitarian weatherman's tool. You'll find one of Anders Lunde's wind-vane whirligigs featured in the wind vane chapter on pages 70-73.

The second and third types, the winged and arm-waving whirligigs, are quite similar to one another. Both types consist of a stationary body of some sort, with—as the names suggest—wings or arms spinning on either side. The spinning Hummingbird, featured on pages 121-123, is a great example of a winged whirligig.

The final type, the mechanical whirligig, requires a little more engineering than the others. But don't be scared by the word "engineering"—you won't need a slide ruler, glasses, or a class in advanced calculus to make one of these fun toys! A mechanical whirligig is basically a machine with a propeller that catches the wind and drives a cam, gear, wheel, or some other device to put the whirligig's parts into motion. The Flag Wavers on pages 94-98, the Centipede on pages 101-105,

and the Early Bird on pages 106-110 are all mechanical whirligigs.

As you can see, wind toys and whirligigs offer the inventive mind endless creative possibilities. The following chapter will give you the instructions to tap into a few of those possibilities, and the inspiration to come up with new ones all your own.

Flag Wavers *Whirligig*

Straightedge

Tape measure

Pencil

Jigsaw

Coping saw

Square

Clamps

Drill

Drill bits (see "Tips")

Hacksaw

Screwdriver

Wood chisel

Small carving knife

Metal shears

Hammer

6/32 thread-cutting die

Paintbrushes

Anders Lunde, the woodworker who made this patriotic whirligig, included a hard-working couple—Uncle and Mrs. Sam—in his design. If you're not from the U.S.A., just modify the project by including your own nation's figures and flag!

Lumber and Hardware

1   Pine 1 x 6, 20" long

1   Pine 2 x 2, 2" long

1   Pine 1 x 2, 8" long

1   Pine 1 x 4, 3½" long

1   Pine 2 x 4, 12" long

1   Pine 1 x 10, 10" long

2   Pieces of ¼" x 1" x 7¾" stock

1   ⅜"-diameter dowel, several inches long

1   Piece of ⅜" x ½" x 17" stock

1   Piece of ³⁄₁₆" x 4" x 24" stock

2   Pieces of ¾" x ¾" x 8" stock

1   ¾"-diameter dowel, 7" long

5   No. 6 x 1½" flathead screws

1   16-penny nail

1   ⅜"-diameter tension pin, 2" long

2   Metal screws, ½" long

2   Angle irons, 1½" size

1   ³⁄₁₆"-diameter brass tubing, 12" long

1   ½" screw eye

1   Piece of sheet aluminum, 12" x 12"

~   Several very small nails

2   6/32 machine screws, 1¾" long

8   Nuts for 6/32 machine screws

1   ⅛"-diameter brass rod, 7¾" long

1   6/32 machine screw, 1½" long

1   ⁵⁄₆₄"-diameter brass rod, 12" long

1   ¾" brad

2   No. 8 brass washers

1   30-penny nail

Supplies

Sandpaper

Wood glue

Exterior paints

Tips

~Beginning woodworkers will find this whirligig a real challenge—possibly a larger one than they'd like to accept! If you're a novice who thinks of mistakes as opportunities to learn, however, go ahead and give it a shot!

~If you don't already own a complete set of drill bits, purchase an inexpensive one; you'll need many different sizes to drill the holes in this project.

~The hardware list for this wind toy is extensive, but don't be dismayed. Use what you have on hand or whatever's readily available at your local hardware store.

~Stationary power saws will make your cutting and shaping jobs much easier. If you don't own these tools, you'll need to have a lumberyard prepare ³⁄₁₆", ¼", and ³⁄₈" stock for you. You'll also need to plan on spending some extra time with your handheld cutting tools.

~The man's body and the woman's body in this project are each 1³⁄₈" thick. You can cut these pieces from 2 x 4 stock and leave them 1½" thick or, if you have the appropriate equipment, you can thin your stock down before cutting the parts.

Figure 1

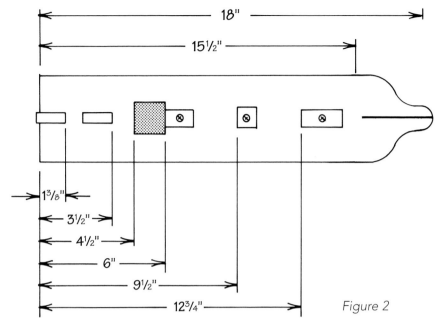

Figure 2

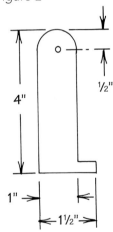

Cutting List

Number	Part Name	Dimensions
1	Platform	¾" x 4" x 18½"
1	Support block	1½" x 1½" x 2"
1	Man's legs	¾" x 1½" x 4"
1	Man's body	1³⁄₈" x 2" x 6½"
1	Woman's skirt	¾" x 2" x 3½"
1	Man's body wedge	⁷⁄₈" x ¾" x ¾"
1	Woman's body	1³⁄₈" x 2" x 5"
4	Arms	¼" x 1" x 7¾"
2	Hand separators	³⁄₈"-diameter dowel, ½" long
1	Flagpole base	¾" x 1" x 2½"
1	Flagpole	³⁄₈" x ½" x 17"
2	Propeller arms	¾" x ¾" x 8"
4	Propeller blades	³⁄₁₆" x 3½" x 6"
1	Circular stand	¾" x 8" diameter
1	Stand tube	¾"-diameter dowel, 7" long

Figure 3

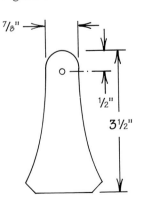

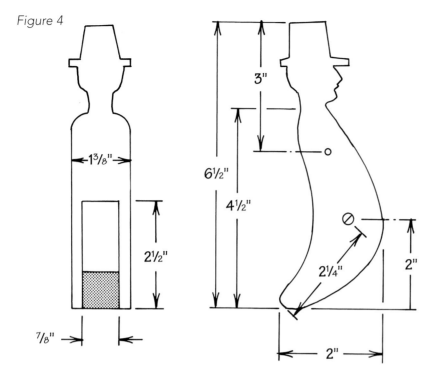

Figure 4

Instructions

1. Using figure 1 (see page 95) as a guide, mark an outline for the platform onto 1 x 6 stock. (Note that the rudder end shouldn't be more than 1" wide.) Cut the platform out and cut a 3½"-long slot in the rudder end. Sand the piece to smooth the cut edges.

2. Mark a centerline down the length of the platform's face. Then mark this face as shown in figure 1, to show the placement of the two angle irons, the man's legs, the flagpole base, and the woman's skirt.

3. On the platform's bottom face, mark the location of the support block (the shaded area in fig. 1) and the three holes for the flathead screws that will attach the man, the flagpole base, and the woman to the upper face. Drill these ⅛" holes now.

4. To make the support block, cut a 2"-long piece from 2 x 2 stock. Drill a

centered ⅜" hole through its length. Attach the block to the bottom of the platform by drilling two ⅛" holes through the upper face of the platform and then turning a couple of No. 6 x 1½" flathead screws through the platform and into the block underneath.

5. Using a hacksaw, cut off the head of a 16-penny nail. Place the nail head over one end of a ⅜"-diameter tension pin to serve as a cap for the pin. Then insert the capped tension pin (cap first) into the hole in the support block.

6. Using ½"-long screws and referring to figure 1, attach the angle irons to the upper face of the platform.

7. Using figure 2 (see page 95) as a guide, sketch the man's legs onto 1 x 2 stock. Then cut the piece out and drill a ³⁄₁₆"-diameter hole through it, ½" from the top. To line this hole, insert a ¾" length of ³⁄₁₆"-diameter brass tubing. Secure the legs to the platform temporarily with a No. 6 screw inserted

through the ⅛" hole in the platform. (You'll adjust the platform pieces before you fasten them permanently.)

8. Using figure 3 (see page 95) as a guide, sketch the woman's skirt onto 1 x 4 stock. Cut the skirt out and drill a ³⁄₁₆" hole through it, ½" from the top. Line the hole with a ¾" length of ³⁄₁₆"-diameter brass tubing. Secure the woman's skirt to the platform temporarily with a No. 6 screw.

9. Using figure 4 as a guide, sketch the man's body onto 2 x 4 stock and then cut it out. (You'll shape the man's head later, so leave plenty of wood in this area for carving.) Next, carefully cut out a ⅞"-wide slot, 2½" deep, in the coattail portion of the body. Then carve a wedge piece (see the shaded area of fig. 4) and secure it into the slot with glue. (In the photo on page 94, the wedge piece is visible behind the propeller blade.) Allow the glue to dry.

10. Using the photo on the opposite page as a guide, drill a ¹⁄₁₆" pilot hole in the top of the coattail wedge piece and insert a ½" screw eye.

11. Using a ⁹⁄₆₄" bit, drill a hole through the side of the man's body, 2¼" back from the tip of the coattail (see fig. 4). Also drill a shoulder hole, using a ⁷⁄₆₄" bit, 3" from the top of the body. Then use a small carving knife to shape the man's head.

12. Using figure 5 as a guide, sketch the woman's body onto 2 x 4 stock and cut it out (leave plenty of wood for carving the head and hat). Then, cut out a ⅞"-wide slot in it, about 1¼" deep at the front of the body and about ⅞" deep at the back. Drill the hip and shoulder holes (see fig. 5), as you did in step 11, using ⁹⁄₆₄" and ⁷⁄₆₄" bits. Then carve out the head and hat.

13. Using figure 6 as a guide, cut out two arm pieces, each 7¾" long, from ¼"-thick stock. Use a ⁷⁄₆₄" bit to drill shoulder holes ⅜" from each end and a hole through the hand portion.

14. Cut out a ¾" x 1" x 2½" flagpole base from 1 x 2 stock. Then cut out a slot in the top, 1" deep and ⅜" wide.

15. Mark and cut out a ⅜" x 17" blank for the flagpole from ⅜"-thick stock. Using a knife, sandpaper, and file, shape and round the pole, starting about 4½" from its base. Then drill two ¼" holes through the ½"-wide edge, ½" and 3½" from the bottom. Also cut a very thin, 2½"-long slot in the tip of the pole for the flag.

16. The flagpole is separated from the hands by two dowel tubes. To make these separators, drill ⅛" holes through two ½"-long pieces of ⅜" dowel.

17. Using metal shears, cut a 2½" x 3¾" flag and a 7" x 5" rudder from the sheet aluminum, shaping the rudder as shown in the photo on page 94. Set the rudder aside. Slip the flag into the flag-pole slot, and mark two points on the flagpole for the very small nails that will secure the flag in place. Then remove the flag and prepare it for the nails by using a small, sharp nail to punch two small holes through the metal. Drill two ¹⁄₃₂" holes at the marks on the flagpole. Return the flag to the slot and drive two small nails through the holes.

18. Mount the man's body onto his legs and the woman's body onto her skirt by inserting 1¾" machine screws and securing them with 6/32 nuts. (Don't tighten the nuts all the way down or the wooden parts won't move.)

19. Position the arm pieces over the holes in the man's and woman's

Figure 5

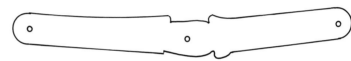

5¼"

⁷⁄₈"

⁷⁄₈"

◄1³⁄₈"►

2"

Figure 6

shoulders. Then slip two 3"-long, ⁵⁄₆₄"-diameter brass rods through the holes. Bend down one end of each rod at a 90° angle to keep it from slipping out. (You'll bend the other end once you've completed all adjustments.)

20. Position the flagpole in the flagpole-base notch and slip a 6/32 machine screw, 1½" long, through the holes. Turn two 6/32 nuts onto the ends. To attach the arm pieces to the flagpole, insert a 3¼"-long, ⁵⁄₆₄"-diameter brass rod through one arm piece, an arm separa-tor, the flagpole, another arm separator, and through the other arm piece. Bend the rod down at one end.

21. To test the assemblage, grip the screw eye in the man's coattails and move it up and

down. The figures and flag should move back and forth without difficulty. Make any adjustments necessary before bending down the straight ends of the three brass rods.

22. To prepare the camshaft for the propeller, use a 6/32 die to cut a 1"-long thread at one end of the 7¾"-long, ⅛"-diameter brass rod. Cut a ¾"-long thread at the other end (the cam end). Then bend a ¾"-deep cam, 1" from the cam end.

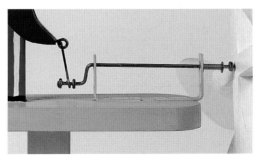

23. Insert the camshaft through the upper holes in the angle irons and turn two 6/32 machine nuts onto the cam end, leaving space between them for the connecting rod. To make the connecting rod, loop a piece of ⁵⁄₆₄" brass rod around the threaded camshaft. Thread the other end through the screw eye in the coattail, adjust the length as necessary, and make a loop in the end of the rod to connect it to the screw eye. When you've finished making any adjustments, secure the two camshaft nuts with waterproof glue.

24. Unfasten the connecting rod, disassemble the parts, and paint them. (Don't forget to paint the rudder!) When the paint is dry, reassemble the parts, using wood glue and No. 6 screws to attach the man's legs, flagpole base, and woman's skirt to the platform. Insert the rudder into the slot in the platform, securing it with glue and a ¾"-long brad driven through the narrow end of the platform. (Punch a hole in the rudder to prepare it for the brad, just as you prepared the flag in step 17.)

25. Cut two ¾" x ¾" x 8" propeller arms. Then, in each arm, use a jigsaw to cut a centered ¾"-wide, ⅜"-deep notch. Trim the notches with a knife if necessary.

26. Take a close look at the project photo and figures 7, 8, and 9. Each propeller blade fits against a flat arm surface that's cut at an angle. To mark the first set of cuts, hold the arms together at their notches to form a lap joint. (Don't glue them together yet.) Now, looking down at the ¾"-square end of an arm, mark a line from corner to corner (see fig. 7). Turn the arms 45° and mark the next arm end in the same fashion, running the line in the same direction. (All the propeller blades must be angled in the same direction!)

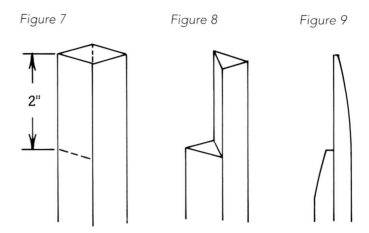

Figure 7 *Figure 8* *Figure 9*

2"

Repeat to mark all four arm ends. Then mark off each arm 2" down from its end.

27. Dismantle the arms and cut out the 2"-long sections from each end (see fig. 8). If you like, you may shape the arms further by carving them as shown in figure 9.

28. Using figure 10 as a guide, cut out four 3½" x 6" propeller blades from ³⁄₁₆"-thick stock, making sure that the bottom edge of each is at least 1" wide.

29. Using wood glue and very small nails, attach the blades to the ends of the propeller arms, bending the nails over on the back. (Drill small pilot holes for the nails, or you may crack the wood.) Then glue the two arms together at the notched lap joint.

30. When the glue has dried, drill a ⁷⁄₆₄" hole through the center of the arm joint. Then paint the propeller as desired and allow the paint to dry.

31. To assemble the propeller and cam shaft, first cut a ⅝"-long sleeve from ³⁄₁₆"-diameter brass tubing. Slip a No. 8 brass washer, the sleeve you just cut, and another No. 8 brass washer onto the cam shaft, where the shaft protrudes

from the front angle iron. (These will keep the propeller from striking the platform.) Then turn the propeller onto the threaded end of the shaft.

32. To make a stand similar to the one shown in the project photo, first cut an 8"-diameter circle from a 1 x 10 and drill a ¾"-diameter hole in its center. Cut a 7"-long piece of ¾"-diameter dowel and glue it into the hole in the circular base. To make a spindle, cut the head off a 30-penny nail. Drill a small hole in the upper end of the dowel and insert the spindle. To mount the whirligig, fit the tension pin in the support block over the top of the spindle.

Figure 10

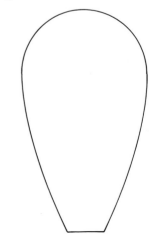

Wind Swirl *Wind Toy*

As it turns slowly around in the breeze, designer Mike Durkin's wind swirl offers a mesmerizing effect, similar to the turning colors of old-fashioned barber poles. The swirl is an easy project to construct, even if you've never used a saw or drill before.

Tools

Tape measure
Pencil
Straightedge
Hand saw or circular saw
Sander
Drill
¼" drill bit
Pliers
Paintbrushes

Lumber and Hardware

30	1 x 2 pine slats, each 12" long
1	"All-thread" rod, 24" x ¼" diameter
3	¼" flat washers
2	¼" lock washers
3	¼" nuts
1	Piece of heavy-grade solid wire, 8" long
1	Dog-chain swivel
1	Length of heavy-gauge chain
1	2" or 3" screw eye or hook

Supplies

Sandpaper
Exterior paints

Tips

~The 1 x 2 pine used in this project is usually sold in 8' lengths, so you'll probably need to buy four lengths.

~Remember that the kerf of your saw blade will eat up a bit of the length of each slat. Your finished slats will each be slightly less than 12" long.

~Be sure to hang the finished project, which is surprisingly heavy, where no one will walk into it by mistake. Accidental encounters could cause serious damage to passers-by!

Instructions

1. Cut the 30 pine slats from the 1 x 2 stock and sand the edges of each piece well.

2. Through the face of each slat, drill a centered ¼"–diameter hole.

3. Slip the slats onto the threaded rod, as shown in figure 1 (see page 100).

4. At the bottom of the assembly, slip a ¼" flat washer and a ¼" lock washer onto the rod. Then tighten a ¼" nut down onto the lock washer.

5. Repeat step 4 at the top of the assembly.

6. Referring to figure 2, use pliers to twist one end of the heavy-gauge wire around the threaded rod at the top of the assembly, just above the nut. To secure the wire in place, slip another ¼" flat washer onto the rod and tighten another ¼" nut down onto the flat washer.

7. Bend the wire upward at a 90° angle and use your pliers to shape a secure loop in the other end.

Figure 1

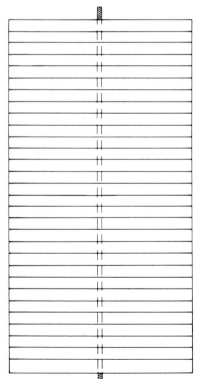

Figure 2

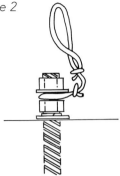

8. Turn the slats on the rod to form a swirl. If necessary, retighten the nuts when you're finished.

9. If you like, you may paint the slats as shown in the project photos. Another way to decorate your swirl is to draw an imaginary line down the center of the swirl as the slats rest flat on your work surface. After turning the slats to form the swirl, paint the exposed surfaces to one side of this line with one color, and those on the other side with another color. Then turn the assembly over and repeat on the other side.

10. Suspend the swirl by fastening one end of a dog-chain swivel to the wire loop and the other end to a rope or chain. (The swivel will allow the swirl to turn freely in the breeze.) Then attach the rope or chain to a sturdy screw eye or hook. This project is heavy, so make sure the screw eye or hook is inserted into a structural timber that can support its weight.

Wind Instruments

Wind is the natural movement of air. When we exhale, we create wind. And when we exhale in a controlled manner into a wind instrument, we create music—the vibrations of air columns forced into the instrument produce tones.

What do you think of when you think of a wind instrument? Perhaps a tuba, flute, or saxophone? You'd be surprised by how many different wind instruments there are; the list that follows includes only a representative sampling.

Bassoon	**Kazoo**	**Tin whistle** (or
Clarinet	**Launedda**	**penny whistle)**
Crumhorn	**Oboe**	**Trombone**
***Didgeridu**	**Ocarina**	**Trumpet**
Double reed	**Panpipes**	**Tuba**
Euphonium	**Pipe organ**	**Uilleann pipes** (or
Flue	****Post horn**	*Irish bagpipe)*
French horn	**Recorder**	
Harmonica	**Saxophone**	

*The didgerido—an Australian aboriginal instrument—is a large bamboo or wooden trumpet.
**The post horn, popular during the eighteenth and nineteenth centuries, is a coiled copper or brass instrument that was blown by the postillions (or guides) of horse-drawn mail coaches.

Centipede *Whirligig & Wind Vane*

A good breeze will set designer Don Shull's creepy-crawly whirligig into a scuttling frenzy, so display this project well away from the neighborhood exterminator.

Tools

Tape measure

Metal file

Drill

$\frac{1}{16}$", $\frac{1}{8}$", $\frac{7}{32}$", $\frac{17}{64}$", $\frac{3}{16}$", and $\frac{1}{4}$" high-speed steel bits

$\frac{5}{8}$" spade bit

Pliers

Hacksaw

Propane torch

6/32 thread-cutting die

Pencil

Jigsaw or coping saw

Paintbrushes

Small carving knife

Screwdriver

Router (optional)

Clamps

Hacksaw or side cutters

Supplies

UHMW plastic, $\frac{3}{8}$" x $\frac{3}{4}$" x 8"

Sandpaper

50/50 solder and flux

Exterior paint

Waterproof glue

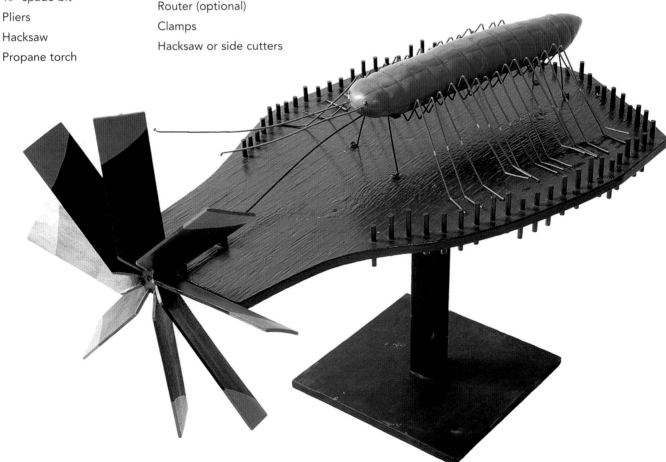

Lumber and Hardware

1	Piece of exterior plywood, ½" x 48" x 48"
11'	¼"-diameter dowel (optional)
~	Wood for centipede body (see step 17)
1	Pine 2 x 2, 8" long
1	Scrap of 1"-thick stock, approx. 4" in diameter
1	Piece of exterior plywood, ⅛" x 8" x 24" (see "Tips")
1	½"-diameter auger bit, about 9½" long (see "Tips")
1	Strip of galvanized steel, ¹⁄₁₆" x ½" x 28"
26"	⅛"-diameter steel rod
30'	12-gauge galvanized wire
24"	³⁄₁₆" (outer diameter), ⅛" (inner diameter) copper tubing
12"	⅛"-diameter steel cable
4	6/32 nuts
4	Sheet metal screws
1	3" x 3" piece of 16-gauge galvanized steel (see "Tips")
1	½"-diameter hex-head bolt, 3½" long
4	No. 6 x ½" hex-head screws
1	No. 8 x 1" wood screw
1	½"-diameter rigid copper tubing, 6½" long
2	No. 6 x 1" wood screws
1	¼"-diameter hex-head bolt, 4" long
1	¼"-20 nut

Tips

~If you're not familiar with the soldering process or with using propane torches, either ask for help at your local hardware store or check out a metalworking book from your library.

~Look for the ½"-diameter auger bit at flea markets or antique stores. These bits come in a variety of sizes; just find the closest match you can and adapt the instructions as necessary.

~UHMW plastic is "ultra-high molecular weight" plastic. It's available in ⅜" x ¾" x 48" strips.

~Take a good look at the photo of the centipede's interior before you tackle this project.

~To make the antennae, you can substitute two bicycle spokes for two 10" lengths of 12-gauge wire.

~A sheet metal shop can cut the 3" x 3" piece of 16-gauge galvanized steel for you.

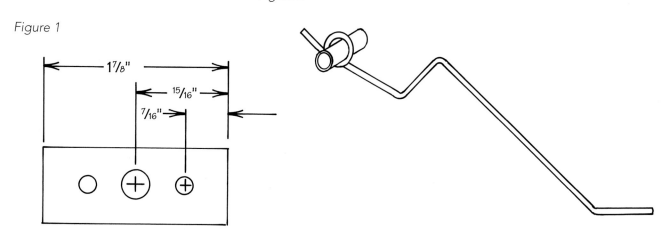

Figure 2

Figure 1

Figure 3

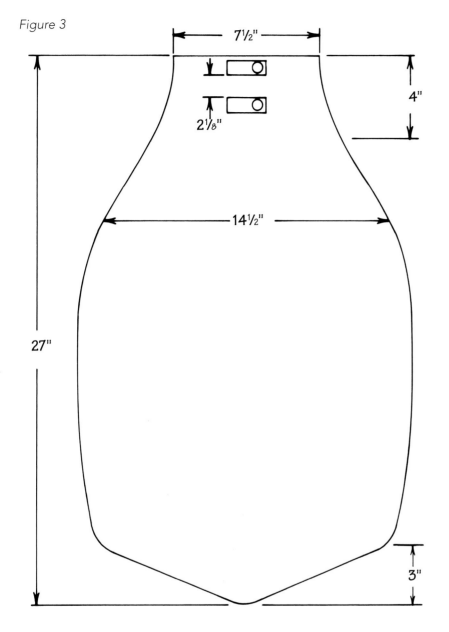

7½"

2⅛"

4"

14½"

27"

3"

Instructions

1. The operation of this whirligig is really quite simple. The motion of the propeller turns a bolt attached to a steel cable, the steel cable turns an auger bit, and the turning auger bit raises and lowers the feet. The ends of the auger bit fit into holes in two plastic end blocks and must be able to turn freely in those holes. Start this project by sanding or filing the auger bit's ends down to

¼" in diameter. Also file the bit's sharp cutting edges to round them off.

2. In the shank end of the auger bit, drill a ⅛"-diameter hole, ½" deep, to receive the steel cable that will transmit the motion of the propeller.

3. Cut two end blocks from the UHMW plastic, each 1⅞" long. In each of these end blocks, drill two ⅛"-diameter holes to accept the steel rods

to which the feet are attached and a ¹⁷⁄₆₄"-diameter hole to accept the ends of the auger bit (see fig. 1).

4. To make the metal frame for the end blocks, auger bit, and rods, first insert the ¼"-diameter ends of the auger bit into the larger holes in the end blocks. Then bend a ¹⁄₁₆"-thick strip of ½"-wide galvanized steel into a rectangle that will fit snugly around the ends blocks (the frame in this project is about 10¾" long), overlapping its ends. Remove the bent steel strip from the bit and blocks, use a hacksaw to cut it to the correct length, and solder its overlapped ends together.

5. In the short ends of the steel frame, drill holes to match those in the end blocks. The holes in the frame and end blocks must be aligned when the frame is in place.

6. Using a hacksaw, cut two pieces of ⅛"-diameter steel rod, each about 1" longer than the frame. Then use a 6/32 die to thread about ½" at both ends of both rods. Once the rods are installed in the end blocks and frame, they must extend far enough on both sides to accept wire brackets and nuts.

7. Next, decide on the number of legs your centipede will have (the centipede shown has 29). With a hacksaw, cut that many 10½" lengths from 12-gauge galvanized wire. Also cut an equal number of short, ³⁄₁₆" (outer diameter) copper tubing sections, each about ¼" long.

8. Using figure 2 and the detail photo on page 105 as guides, wrap one end of each wire leg around one of the short sections of copper tubing, bending the leg as shown. Then solder the leg to the tubing. Note that the short portion of the leg will "ride" under the turning auger bit; as the bit turns in the wind, its raised edges will move the legs up and down.

9. To create separators that will keep the legs from sliding together on the rods, cut approximately 30 additional lengths of the ³⁄₁₆" (outer diameter) copper tubing, each ³⁄₈" long.

10. Solder a length of ¹⁄₈"-diameter steel cable into the hole in the auger bit. Then insert the auger bit into the end blocks and set the blocks and bit into the frame.

11. Insert the two ¹⁄₈"-diameter steel rods through the holes in one end of the frame. Then thread the soldered leg tubes and separators onto the rods before pushing the rods through the holes in the opposite end of the frame. Turn a 6/32 nut onto each threaded rod end to keep the rods temporarily in place.

12. To make the platform, first position the metal frame and legs on a piece of exterior plywood. Then use figure 3 on page 103 as a guide to sketch a platform shape onto the plywood, about 27" long and 17" wide. (Make sure the platform isn't too long to allow a connection between the steel cable and propeller.) Remove the frame and cut the platform out with a jigsaw or coping saw. To add the optional dowels around the platform edges, drill ¼"-diameter holes (this project has 62) through the plywood and glue 2" lengths of ¼"-diameter dowel into them.

13. Paint the platform as desired and allow the paint to dry.

14. To make the two brackets that raise the frame and legs above the platform, first remove the temporary 6/32 nuts from the ¹⁄₈"-diameter rods. Then, referring to figure 4, bend two lengths of 12-gauge galvanized wire, looping the wire around the rod ends as shown and forming eyelets at each end. The front bracket should raise the frame about 3" from the platform; the rear bracket should raise it about 2". Replace the 6/32 nuts and tighten them down securely to hold the brackets onto the frame.

15. Fasten the brackets to the platform by driving sheet metal screws through the eyelets and into the platform.

16. Check to see that the outermost bends in the feet touch the platform. Also turn the auger bit by hand and make sure that each foot is lifted and dropped as the bit turns. Adjust the feet as necessary by bending them.

17. The carved centipede body has a rectangular hollow in it that allows the body to fit snugly over the frame. There are two ways to make this body: the easiest is to glue up five pieces of wood to form a hollow box with a bottom and four sides. If you choose this method, be sure to frame up these pieces so that the hollow in them is barely larger than the metal frame. It's also possible to route out a rectangular hollow in a 14½"-long piece of 1¾" x 2½" stock.

18. Using a small carving knife, shape the exterior of the body and sand any rough spots to smooth them. To add antennae, drill two ¹⁄₁₆"-diameter holes in one end of the body and insert two bicycle spokes or two 10" lengths of 12-gauge galvanized wire. Paint the body as desired and allow the paint to dry.

19. To elevate the platform while you finish working on the project, it's best to build the whirligig stand now. Start by drilling four, equally spaced, ³⁄₁₆"-diameter holes in a 3" x 3" square of 16-gauge galvanized sheet metal. Then solder the head of a ½"-diameter, 3½"-long hex-head bolt to the metal square's center.

Figure 4

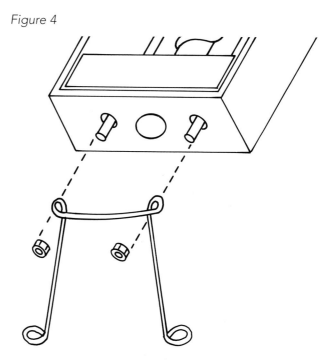

20. Find the platform's balance point by positioning it on top of a dowel until it doesn't tip. Then, at the balance point, fasten the metal square to the bottom of the platform with four No. 6 x ½" hex-head sheet metal screws.

21. To make the stand, cut a 10½" x 10½" base from ½"-thick plywood. Then attach an 8"-long 2 x 2 to its center by driving a No. 8 x 1" wood screw up through the plywood. Drill a centered ⅝"-diameter, 2"-deep hole into the 2 x 2 and slip a 6½"-long piece of ½"-diameter rigid copper tubing into the hole. Finally, fit the bolt that extends from the platform into the copper tube. The platform should turn freely on the stand.

22. To make the propeller hub, use a jigsaw to cut a 1½"-diameter circle from 1"-thick wood. Drill a ⁷⁄₃₂"-diameter hole through its center. On the circle's face, make eight equidistant marks around the circumference. Then, at each mark, use a coping saw to cut eight ⅛"-wide, ⅜"-deep slots in the rim, each angled at 45°.

23. Cut eight rectangular propellers from ⅛"-thick plywood or craft wood, each 7" long x 2" wide. As you can see in the project photo on page 101, Don has cut off one front corner of each blade. If you'd like to do the same, "dry-fit" each blade into a slot, mark the point at which the blade emerges from the slot, remove the blades and, at each mark, cut the blade at an angle. Glue the blades into the slots. When the glue has dried, paint the propeller as desired.

24. To connect the steel cable to the propeller, first cut two mounting blocks from UHMW plastic, each 1⅛" long. On the ¾"-wide face of each block, make a mark ⁷⁄₁₆" from one short end and ⁷⁄₁₆" from one long edge. Then drill a ¹⁷⁄₆₄" hole at each mark.

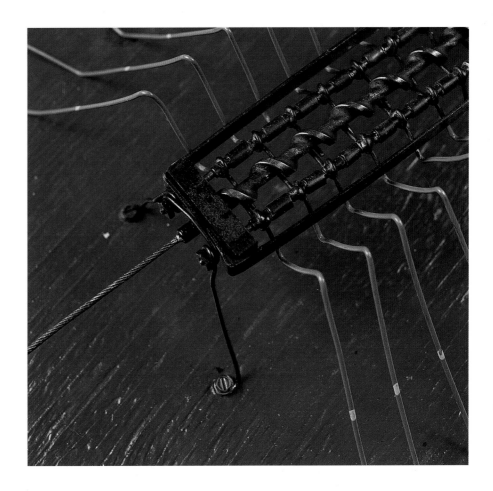

25. Position the mounting blocks on the platform as shown in figure 3 (see page 103). Attach them by pre-drilling holes and driving a 1"-long wood screw through the exposed long edge of each one, into the platform.

26. Drill a centered ⅛"-diameter, ½"-deep hole into the head of the ¼"-diameter hex-head bolt. Then, to check how long the steel cable should be, slip the bolt through the holes in the mounting blocks and draw the cable up next to the bolt head. Mark the cable and cut it with a hacksaw or side cutters, about ½" beyond the mark.

27. Remove the bolt from the mounting blocks and solder the free cable end into the hole in the bolt head. Slip the bolt back into the mounting blocks.

28. Turn a ¼"-20 nut onto the threaded end of the bolt, as far as the nut will go. Then turn the threaded end of the bolt into the propeller hub and back up the nut until it tightens against the hub. (The nut helps lock the propeller onto the bolt.)

The Early Bird *Whirligig*

Poor Mr. Rooster—he set his alarm clock early, he struggled from the roost at the break of day, and yet he still can't seem to get that darn worm. Well, his plight will be your pleasure because you're sure to chuckle every time you watch designer Mike Durkin's ravenous rooster work for breakfast.

Tools

- Straightedge
- Tape measure
- Pencil
- Square
- Compass
- Jigsaw
- Coping saw
- Clamps
- Paintbrushes
- Drill
- 1/16" and 1/4" drill bits
- 1 1/2" spade bit
- 1/4" wood chisel or sharp knife
- Hammer
- Screwdriver
- Pliers
- Cutting pliers
- Hot-melt glue gun

Supplies

- Sandpaper
- Exterior paints
- Wood glue
- Flat rubber band or rubber fishing worm, approx. 13" long
- Hot glue sticks

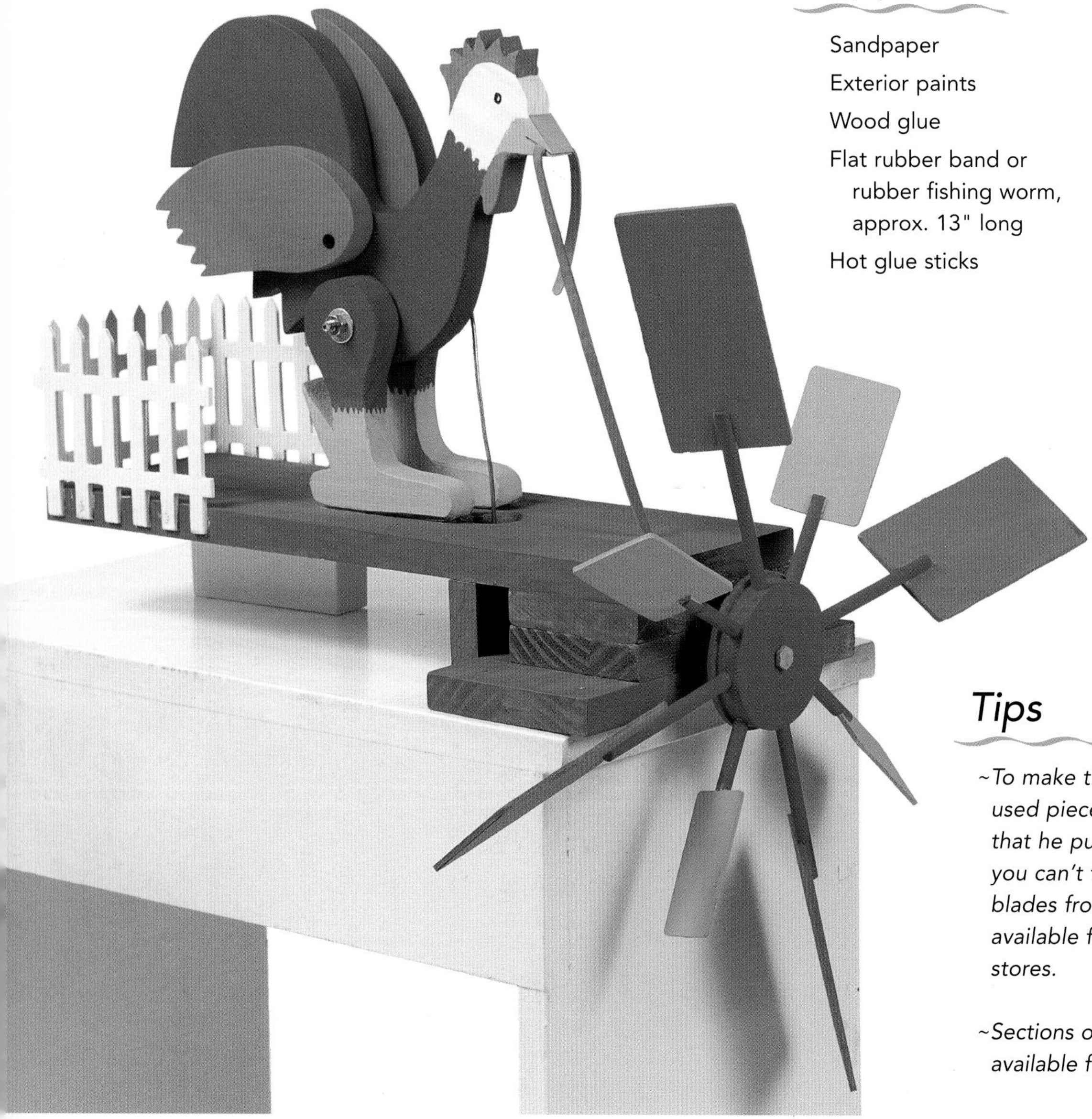

Tips

~ To make the propeller blades, Mike used pieces of precut craft wood that he purchased at a craft store. If you can't find these, you can cut the blades from a sheet of thin plywood, available from many building-supply stores.

~ Sections of craft-wood fencing are available from craft stores.

Lumber and Hardware

1	Pine 1 x 12, 3' long
1	Piece of ⅛"-thick plywood, 12" x 12" (see "Tips")
1	¼"-diameter dowel, 30" long
1	¼"-diameter machine bolt, 8" long
1	Piece of scrap wood, ¾" x 2" x 5½"
3	Pieces of craft fencing, 5½" x 4¼" tall
1	¼"-diameter machine bolt, 8" long
1	Box No. 6 finishing nails
8	1¼" drywall screws
7	¼" flat metal washers
4	¼" nuts
2	¾" drywall screws
1	¼"-diameter machine bolt, 3" long
1	Piece of heavy-gauge solid wire, 7½" long
1	Flathead nail
6	¼" brads
4	Galvanized wood screws for mounting

Cutting List

Number	Part Name	Dimensions
1	Base A	¾" x 5½" x 17½"
2	Base B	¾" x 3½" x 5½"
1	Mounting plate	¾" x 4½" x 9½"
1	Propeller hub	¾" x 3" diameter
1	Hub A	¾" x 2" diameter
1	Hub B	¾" x 1½" diameter
2	Legs	See figure 2
1	Body	See figure 3
2	Wings	See figure 4
4	Propeller blades	⅛" x 5⅜" x 2⅝" (see "Tips")
4	Propeller blades	⅛" x 2" x 3" (see "Tips")
1	Brace	¾" x 2" x 5½"

Figure 1

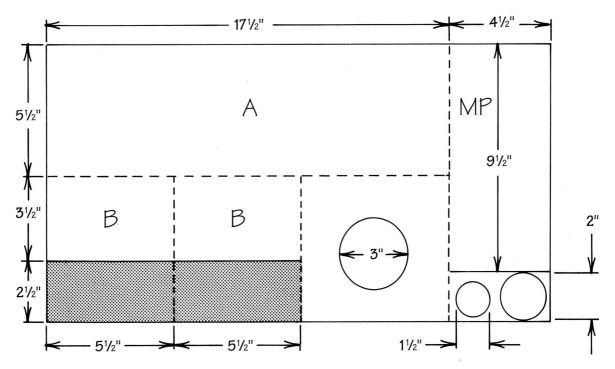

Instructions

1. Cut a 22" length from the 1 x 12 and mark it as shown in figure 1 (see page 107). Then cut out all these pieces with a jigsaw or coping saw. Sand the edges of each piece well.

2. Photocopy the wing, leg, and body patterns shown in figures 2, 3, and 4, enlarging them to the dimensions shown. Transfer the pattern outlines to the remaining length of 1 x 12 and cut them out with a jigsaw or coping saw; then sand the edges well. (You'll need to juggle the pattern pieces on the stock, but they will fit!)

3. If you haven't been able to find precut rectangles of craft wood to use as propeller blades, cut these blades now from ⅛"-thick plywood. (See the "Cutting List" for their dimensions.)

4. Cut the ¼"-diameter dowel into eight propeller blade shafts: four 2½" long and four 4½" long. Then, using a coping saw and referring to figure 5, cut a ⅞"-deep notch in one end of each 4½"-long shaft and a ½"-deep notch in one end of each 2½"-long shaft.

5. Paint all the wooden whirligig parts as desired and let them dry thoroughly.

6. Using wood glue, attach one large blade to each of the long blade shafts, and one small blade to each of the short blade shafts. Clamp the shafts and blades together until the glue has dried.

7. On the rim of the 3" propeller hub, measure and mark eight centered, equidistant holes. Then use a drill and ¼"-diameter drill bit to bore a ½"-deep hole at each mark. Also drill a ¼"-diameter hole through the center of the propeller hub.

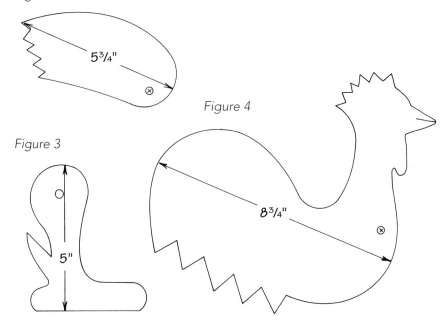

Figure 2

5¾"

Figure 4

Figure 3

5"

8¾"

8. Glue a propeller shaft into each of the eight rim holes, angling the blades and alternating the large and small ones as shown in the project photo. (The blade angle should be between 45° and 60°.)

9. Mark a point on the face of the base A piece, 6¼" back from one end and 2¾" from either long edge. Using a spade bit, drill a 1½"-diameter hole through the board at that point.

10. The 8" machine bolt that serves as the propeller shaft runs through a ½"-deep, ¼"-wide channel in the lower base B piece (see fig. 6). To make this channel, first mark two parallel lines across one of the base B pieces, each 2⅝" from a short end. (The lines should be ¼" apart.) Then, using a coping saw to make repeated parallel cuts right next to each other, cut out the channel. Use a chisel or sharp knife to remove any excess wood from the channel.

11. Place the ¾" x 2" x 5½" brace on your work surface, with its long edges running horizontally. Then measure and mark a point 2¾" from either short end and 1⅛" down from the long upper edge. At this mark, drill a ¼"-diameter hole through the wood.

12. Referring to figure 6 again, use wood glue and No. 6 finishing nails to assemble the base A piece and the two base B pieces.

13. Align one long edge of the mounting plate with the front edge of the glued assembly, and fasten the plate to the lower base B plate by driving four 1¼" drywall screws through the plate and into the lower base B piece. (Be careful not to drive the screws through the channel.)

14. Attach the brace piece with No. 6 finishing nails, driving three through the base A piece and into the upper edge of the brace, and two through the brace and into the edge of the mounting plate.

Figure 5

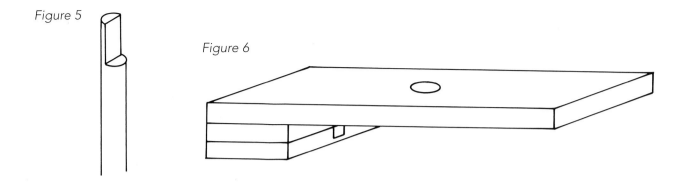

Figure 6

15. Drill a ¼"-diameter hole through the center of hub A.

16. Using figure 7 as a guide, slip the following parts onto the 8"-long machine bolt: the propeller hub, a ¼" flat metal washer, hub A, and another ¼" flat washer. Then slide the end of the bolt through the channel in the lower base B piece and the hole in the brace. Slip a ¼" flat washer over the end of the bolt, and tighten two nuts down onto the washer.

17. After drilling a ¹⁄₁₆"-diameter pilot hole, insert a ¾" drywall screw into the face of hub B, as shown in figure 7. (Don't tighten the screw all the way down.) Then place some wood glue on the end of the threads of the 8" machine bolt and tighten the hub down onto the nuts.

18. Using your coping saw, cut a ¾"-deep slit in the rooster beak to accommodate the rubber worm.

19. Using figure 4 as a guide, insert a ¾" drywall screw into the rooster's body, leaving a few of the threads exposed. You'll hook a length of heavy-gauge wire around this screw in step 25.

20. The rooster body and legs are joined with a 3" machine bolt, as shown in figure 8 (see page 110). If you

own a drill press, bore the ¼"-diameter holes for this bolt by first clamping a rooster leg to each side of the rooster body and aligning the legs evenly so the rooster will stand when the legs are attached. Then drill a hole through the three clamped parts. If you don't own a drill press, clamp the legs together and drill a hole through them first. Then mark and drill a hole through the body.

21. Run the 3" machine bolt through the holes in the legs and body, inserting a ¼" flat metal washer between the head of the bolt and one leg, and another washer between each leg and the body. Slip a washer over the threaded end of the bolt and tighten a nut down onto it. The rooster body must be able to move freely between the legs, so allow for some play when you tighten this bolt.

22. Fasten a rooster wing to each side of the body with a 1¼" drywall screw.

23. Place some glue on the bottom of each rooster leg. Then position the rooster on the assembled base with its feet at the back edge of the 1½" hole. To secure the rooster to the base, insert a 1¼" drywall screw through the bottom of base A and up into each rooster leg.

24. The turning motion of the propeller is transmitted to the rooster body by a length of heavy-gauge wire that is attached both to the body and to hub B. First use cutting pliers to cut a 7½" length of wire. Bend a loop at one end and hook this loop around the head of the drywall screw in hub B. Tighten the screw down to hold the wire in place.

Figure 7

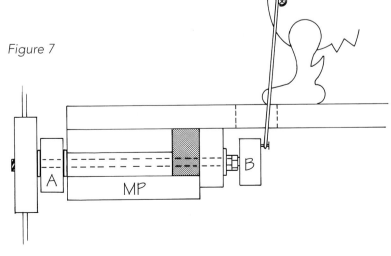

Figure 8

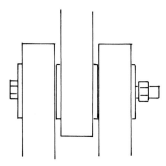

25. Thread the other end of the wire up through the hole in base A and loop it around the drywall screw in the rooster body as shown in figure 7. Trim away any excess wire and tighten down the screw in the body.

26. Slip one end of the rubber band or fishing worm into the slit in the rooster's beak. (Use hot glue if necessary to hold it in place.) To fasten the other end of the worm to the base assembly, first drill a centered ½"-deep, ¼"-diameter hole in base A, 1¾" from the front end. Tuck the loose end of the worm into this hole and use a flathead nail to secure it inside the bottom.

27. Fasten the three lengths of craft fence to the rear of base A with brads.

28. Touch up any scratched paint.

29. To mount the rooster on a fence post or porch rail, drill two pilot holes down through each side of the face of the mounting plate, and fasten the whirligig to the post or rail with galvanized wood screws.

Wind in Language

We all know what wind is, right? That wonderful stuff that unfurls flags and fills billowing sails; that nuisance that ruffles our hair and whips our hemlines too high; that terror that howls down from the hills on cold winter nights. Well, yes. But in English, and in many other languages as well, wind is

~*what we'd like to take out of that pompous co-worker's sails when he starts boasting about his accomplishments at the annual meeting. After all, everyone knows he's a "windbag."*

~*the hint of what's to come when we sense something "in the wind" and the news that we finally we hear when we "get wind" of someone's plans.*

~*the cash we manage to gather when we "raise the wind." If we're lucky, we don't have to raise the wind at all; we run into a "windfall."*

~*that miraculous helping of energy we get after we've run five agonizing miles and suddenly "get our second wind."*

~*something we toss carelessly aside when we're feeling especially brave (or foolhardy) and "toss caution to the winds."*

~*the cue we seek when we're trying to figure out "which way the wind is blowing."*

~*that dreadful feeling we get when we feel "an ill wind" blowing, and know that all is not well with the world.*

~*the nervous, frightened reaction we experience when we "get the wind up."*

~*the mysterious and influential force we sense when we're aware of "the winds of change."*

~*the breath that a tackle on a football team "knocks out of" a player of the opposing team.*

~*the idle talk that we scorn when we tell someone that what he's just said is "a lot of wind."*

~*the martini we wish we hadn't slurped down when we suddenly realize we're "three sheets to the wind."*

Pretty powerful stuff, this wind. Mysterious keeper of secrets, bearer of good and bad news, beneficent and malign—a force that permeates our language as completely as it does our natural environment.

Spinning Tulips *Wind Toy*

Supplies

Sandpaper
Wood glue
Exterior paints

Bright as springtime, but more enduring, designer Robin Clark's garden of spinning tulips will brighten any porch rail or flower bed all year round.

Tools

Tape measure
Straightedge
Pencil
Jigsaw or coping saw
Clamps
Drill
⅛", ⅜", and ⁷⁄₁₆" drill bits
Paintbrushes
Metal file
Hammer

Lumber and Hardware

~for five tulips and one base

1	Piece of ¼"-thick plywood, approx. 7" x 15"
1	Pine 1 x 6, 48" long
1	Pine 2 x 6, 17" long
1	⅜"-diameter dowel, 48" long
10	¾" brads
5	2½" 8-penny nails

Cutting List

Number	Part Name	Dimensions
5	Full petals	¼" x 2¼" x 2½"
10	Half petals	¼" x 1" x 2½"
5	Leaf sets	See step 3

Tips

~The designer used FSC-certified cedar (certified by the Forest Stewardship Council) for parts of this project, but white pine will work just as well.

~Each red tulip is made with three pieces of plywood: one full petal that is U-shaped and two half petals that are glued to the full petal.

Instructions

1. Make a photocopy of figure 1, enlarging it until the petal shape is approximately 2½" tall. Then transfer the petal outline, ten times, to the piece of plywood. To five of the marked outlines, add the parallel dotted lines that run through the center of the pattern.

2. Using a jigsaw or coping saw, cut out the ten pieces and set five of them (these will be the full petals) aside. To make the half petals, cut the remaining five petals along the dotted lines, discarding the thin strip of wood between each pair.

3. Using the project photos as guides, sketch five leaf sets on the 1 x 6 stock. Make each one roughly U-shaped, about 5" wide, and between 7½" and 10" tall. Be creative, giving each set of leaves its own personality, but make sure that the inner bottom edge of each "U" is at least 1¼" wide.

4. Using a jigsaw or coping saw, cut out each leaf set.

5. Cut the 48"-long dowel into five stems, varying their lengths slightly.

6. Sand the edges of all the pieces to a smooth finish.

7. With a drill and ⅛"-diameter bit, drill a centered 1"-deep hole into the bottom edge of each full petal. Also drill a ⅛"-diameter hole, 1" deep, into one end of each dowel stem.

8. To form the individual tulip blossoms, glue a half petal to each face of each full petal. Allow the glue to dry completely.

9. With a drill and a ⅜" bit, drill a centered hole all the way through the base of each leaf set.

10. Apply glue to the inside of the hole in a leaf set. Slide the nondrilled end of a dowel stem through the hole so about 1" protrudes from the bottom of the leaf set. Wipe off any excess glue and secure the stem in place by driving a brad through each face of the leaf set and into the stem. Repeat to attach the remaining stems to the other leaf sets.

11. Paint the tulips and leaf sets as desired.

12. Using a file, remove the heads of the 8-penny nails and taper the headless ends. Fit a nail into the hole in each stem. Then fit the hole in the bottom of each flower over the exposed end of the nail. The flowers should spin easily on the nails; if they don't, widen the holes in the full petals or file the nails to make them narrower.

Figure 1

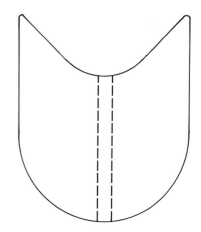

13. In one face of the 2 x 6 base, drill five holes, each ⁷⁄₁₆" in diameter and about 1⅛" deep. Position these holes so that once the flower stems are inserted in them, the flowers will be attractively arranged on the base.

14. Plant your new tulip garden by inserting the protruding end of a dowel stem into each hole in the base.

15. Display your new tulip garden wherever the breeze will be strong enough to spin the flower petals.

Pinwheel Panache *Wind Toys*

A fantastic world of color and motion awaits you with these delightful polymer clay pinwheels, designed by artist Sheila Sheppard. Brighten a yard, path, or porch with their glorious colors, or make them as one-of-a-kind gifts to share with friends and family.

Materials and Supplies

~for one pinwheel

Cernit polymer clay in contrasting colors (see "Tips")

Talcum powder

Metallic powders (optional; see "Tips")

Quick-drying glue

Toothpicks

⅛"-diameter dowel, 12" to 16" long

2" T-pin or 2" wire nail with head

Parchment paper (for baking)

Acrylic paints

3 mm to 4 mm seed bead (see "Tips")

Large unlined index cards (optional)

Telephone wire in several colors (optional)

⅛"-wide plastic ribbon strips or raffia, in several colors (optional)

Tips

~If you've never worked with polymer clay before, start out by reading the basic instructions on pages 18-19. You can certainly make the various parts of these pinwheels with single colors of clay, but if you'd like to try your hand at creating multicolored "canes," the basic instructions will show you how.

~Sheila has found that Cernit polymer clay is the only type with the high flexible tensile strength required to make this project.

~Metallic powders are available from clay suppliers in a range of colors including bronze and silver. They lend an iridescent look to the surface of baked polymer clay.

~The hole in the seed bead must fit loosely around the T-pin or nail. You may want to substitute a hand-shaped and pierced polymer clay bead instead.

~Before you begin, make a photocopy of figure 1 on page 114, enlarging it to 4" x 4".

Figure 1

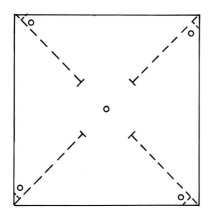

Figure 2

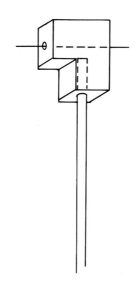

Tools

- Ruler
- Soft-haired paintbrush or makeup brush
- Rolling pin or pasta machine
- Large, ovenproof glass baking dish
- Conventional oven
- Oven thermometer
- Timer
- Pencil
- Craft knife
- Piercing tool or large craft needle
- Scissors
- 8" x 8" plywood work board, with a small finishing nail protruding from its center
- Small paintbrushes
- Wire cutters
- Slicing blade or single-edged razor (optional)
- Hole punch (optional)

Instructions

Preparing the Pinwheel

1. To make multicolored pinwheel heads, start by combining several colors of well-conditioned clay. Stack them, twist them loosely together, and press them together well. You may also want to make some multicolored canes at this time to use in steps 23 and 26.

2. Using a soft-haired brush, dust the your rolling pin or pasta machine with talcum powder. Then roll the clay out into a very thin sheet, slightly larger than the 4"-square pinwheel pattern shown in figure 1. (A pasta machine set at #6 or #7 works well.) Save any clay scraps to use later.

3. After dusting your fingers with talcum powder, lift the sheet and place it in the bottom of the baking dish. Working from the center of the sheet outward, carefully smooth away any visible bubbles. (For added decoration,

you may dust the bottom of the baking dish with metallic powders before placing the clay in the dish and then dust the top of the clay as well.)

4. Bake the clay in a preheated oven, according the clay manufacturer's instructions. Be sure to use an oven thermometer and timer.

5. Let the clay sheet cool thoroughly. If you plan to use the baking dish to bake more clay sheets, let it cool first, too. Never place raw clay on a hot glass surface!

6. Place the enlarged photocopy of figure 1 on top of the baked clay sheet and, using a pencil, trace its outline onto the clay. Check the 4" x 4" dimensions with a ruler. Then, using a craft knife, cut out the square of clay, saving any scraps.

7. Using a pencil, mark diagonal lines on the baked clay square, as shown in figure 1. Mark the center point, where these lines would intersect, with a clearly visible dot. Using a piercing tool, make a hole through the dot; the hole should be large enough to allow the pinwheel to spin loosely on the T-pin or nail that will form the shaft.

8. Using scissors or a craft knife, cut along the marked diagonal lines to within ¾" of the hole in the center, as shown by the dotted lines in figure 1.

9. In figure 1, you'll see a small hole marked in each corner, just to the right of the ends of each diagonal line. Mark these four holes on your baked clay square, taking care not to place them too close to its edges. Then pierce holes at the dots, just as you did at the dot in the center of the square. (These holes, incidentally, can rest to the right or left of the diagonal cuts, as long as all four holes rest on the same sides of their respective diagonals.)

10. Figure 1 also shows four very short lines right next to the four holes you just made. Cut along these four dotted lines to remove a portion of each pointed tip from the pinwheel.

11. Place the clay square on your 8" x 8" workboard, slipping the hole in the center over the finishing nail in the board.

12. Place a very small amount of quick-drying glue around the center hole, being careful not to get glue in the hole itself. Then quickly fold over one of the four pinwheel tips, slipping the hole in it over the workboard nail. Using a toothpick, hold the clay tip down onto the glue around the center hole for a minute or two.

13. Repeat step 12 to fold over the remaining three tips, one at a time, slipping their holes over the nail as before and gluing them securely in place.

Preparing the Handle and Pinwheel Housing

14. Cut the ⅛"-diameter dowel to a comfortable handle length. Then lightly notch or roughen about ½" at one end. This will give the raw clay something to hang onto when you bake the clay pinwheel housing onto the dowel handle.

15. To make a clay housing for the top of the handle (see fig. 2), first condition a ball of clay about 1" in diameter. Then use your hands to mold it into a shape similar to the one shown in the illustration, which is 1" tall.

16. Referring to figure 2, use one end of the dowel to poke a ½"-deep hole into the bottom extension of the

clay housing, rotating the dowel as you do. Don't make this hole too deep. Leave the end of the dowel in the clay, packing the clay tightly around it to hold it in place.

17. Use your piercing tool to make a hole all the way through the upper portion of the clay housing (see fig. 2). Rotate the tool as you do this. Check to see that the hole is large enough by inserting your T-pin or nail through it. If the hole is too tight, your pinwheel won't spin freely.

18. Remove the T-pin or nail and set the housing and handle down on a long piece of parchment paper.

19. You may want to add a decorative clay piece to the bottom of the handle, too. Just roughen this end of the dowel, shape your clay as desired, poke a hole in it with the dowel, and pack the clay tightly around the dowel end.

20. Bake the dowel and the clay at its ends in a preheated oven, according to the clay manufacturer's instructions.

21. When the housing and dowel have cooled, test the pinwheel head by slipping it onto the T-pin or nail, inserting the pin or nail in the hole in the housing, and spinning the pinwheel a few times.

22. Using a small paintbrush, stain the wooden pinwheel shaft with diluted acrylic paints.

Preparing the Pinwheel Shaft

23. As you can see in the project photos, a small piece of clay rests on top of the pinwheel head. To make this piece, first condition a ½"-diameter ball of clay, then shape it into a cone, sphere, or square. Alternatively, you may use a thin slicing blade or single-edged razor to slice a piece of clay from a cane.

Figure 3

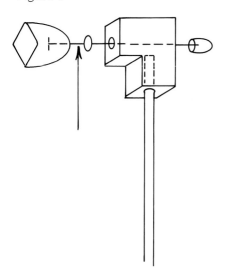

24. Take a good look at figure 3; the arrow indicates where the pinwheel will fit on the T-pin or nail shaft. Insert the pin or nail into the clay piece you've just formed, embedding the head of the T-pin or the head of the nail in the clay. (If you're using a T-pin, you may need to create a small pocket in the clay first by carving out a slice of clay with a craft knife.) Then flatten out what will be the visible front surface of the clay shape.

25. When your pinwheel is assembled, the T-pin or nail is held in place by a ¼"-long conical clay bead on its pointed end. Make this bead now; then use the T-pin or nail to make a hole about halfway through it.

26. With the baked scrap clay you've set aside (see step 6), make embellishments to glue onto your pinwheel. (You may also cut these from baked cane slices.) Sheila has punched out small clay circles with a hole punch. She has also cut narrow strips, triangles, and other shapes from the baked clay scraps and has glued them on to embellish the finished, assembled pinwheel (see step 30).

27. Place the conical bead, the piece you made in step 23, and any clay embellishments that you haven't baked yet on index cards or a piece of parchment paper and bake them in the oven with their flat sides down. (For a glossy rather than matte finish, bake the pieces face down on a glass baking sheet instead.)

Assembling the Pinwheel

28. Using figure 3 as a guide, insert the T-pin or nail (along with the clay shape attached to it) through the hole in the pinwheel. Next slip a seed bead onto the nail. Then insert the pin into the hole in the clay housing. About ¼" of the T-pin or nail should protrude from the back of the housing. If too much protrudes, snip off the excess with wire cutters.

29. Insert the protruding pin or nail into the cone bead and check to see that the pinwheel turns freely. Then glue the cone bead permanently in place on the end of the T-pin or nail.

30. Glue your baked clay embellishments to the pinwheel. As you can see in the photo on page 113, Sheila sometimes wraps narrow plastic ribbon strips with telephone wire and glues these to her pinwheels as well.

Aeolian Harps

magine a harp that plays music without the touch of human hands. It does exist! The Aeolian harp, an instrument with ancient origins, is a loosely-strung, box-shaped harp that is "played" by breezes running across its strings. These stretched gut strings are tuned to play in unison, so as the wind rises and falls away, so do their harmonies.

Named for its mythological player, the Greek god of the wind Aeolus, the Aeolian harp has fascinated people for centuries. Its beautiful and oddly magical music was even described by Aristotle, who believed that Aeolus plucked the harps' strings when he flew across the earth with the Muses in his arms. (The Muses were the nine goddesses of music, poetry, arts and sciences.) According to Aristotle, when Aeolus stroked the strings of this god-designed harp, he played the music of the earth itself.

This wind-played harp was very popular during the eighteenth century (the famous English poet Coleridge entitled one of his poems "the Aeolian Harp") and during the Romantic era, the poet Shelley wrote about the harp as well. Aeolian harps are still made today. When set on a breezy window sill, their strings fill the air with wonderful music.

Old-Fashioned *Windmill*

This classic windmill, made by Robin Clark, not only serves as a wind vane (its upper portion turns to face the wind), but is also designed to fit into the top of a 15"-square planter box so plants can climb up its base.

Materials

Wood glue
Sandpaper

Lumber and Hardware

4'	¾" x 1½" stock
23'	¾" x ¾" stock
1'	¾" x 2¼" stock
1'	¾" x 3¼" stock
1'	¾" x 2½" stock
2'	⅞" x 1½" stock
2'	½" x 3¾" stock
2'	½" x 4½" stock
1'	⅞" x 2¾" stock
5	¼"-diameter dowels, 1½" long
14	1½" drywall screws
32	1" drywall screws
2	¼" carriage bolts, 3" long
6	¼" flat metal washers
2	¼" nuts

Tools

Pencil
Tape measure
Straightedge
Square
Jigsaw or coping saw
Drill
⅛" and ¼" drill bits
Screwdriver

Tips

~Many of the pieces for this project are ¾" thick—the standard thickness of "1 by" lumber that's sold at lumberyards. If you don't own the stationary power tools necessary for making the ½" and ⅞" stock, either substitute ¾" stock for the ⅞"-thick wood and ½"-thick plywood for the ½"-thick stock, or have a local lumberyard

plane your boards to the correct thickness. You can rip your boards to width with a circular saw or jigsaw or have a lumberyard do this job for you.

~If you don't use cedar, you may want to give your finished project a couple of coats of polyurethane spar varnish to protect the wood from the elements.

Cutting List

Number	Part Name	Dimensions
~Rigging		
4	Base pieces	¾" x 1½" x 10"
4	Long verticals	¾" x ¾" x 28½"
2	Wide caps	¾" x 2¼" x 3⅜"
2	Narrow caps	¾" x 2¼" x 2¼"
4	Center verticals	¾" x ¾" x 18½"
4	Bottom cross pieces	¾" x ¾" x 9¼"
4	Top cross pieces	¾" x ¾" x 7"
1	Big top	¾" x 3¼" x 3¼"
1	Small top	¾" x 2½" x 2½"
~Rotor		
5	Rotor blades	½" x 4½" x 13¼"
1	Arrow	⅞" x 1½" x 21½"
1	Feather	½" x 3¾" x 14"
1	Hub	⅞" x 2¾" x 2¾"

Figure 1

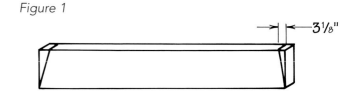

3⅛"

Figure 2

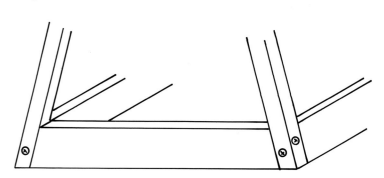

Instructions

1. Begin by marking and cutting all the rigging pieces described in the "Cutting List." (Don't worry about cutting any angles yet.)

2. To cut the angles at the ends of the four base pieces, first mark a point ⅜" in from each short end and draw a line from that mark to the corner above (see fig. 1). Then use a coping saw or jigsaw to cut along the lines.

3. Repeat step 2 to cut angles at both ends of each wide and narrow cap piece.

4. Position a long vertical piece next to the end of a base piece and drill a ⅛"-diameter pilot hole; then glue and screw the two pieces together with a 1" drywall screw. Repeat to fasten all four verticals to the four base pieces (see fig. 2).

5. To assemble the cap that will be attached to the top of the rigging, drill four ⅛"-diameter pilot holes through the face of each wide cap; then secure the wide caps to the narrow caps with 1½" drywall screws (see fig. 3, which also shows the cap attachment process described in the next step).

6. Place the assembled cap over the upper ends of the long verticals. Then drill two ⅛"-diameter pilot holes through each narrow cap piece and drive 1½" drywall screws through them and into the verticals (see fig. 3).

7. Measure and mark a point 3⅜" up from the bottom of a center vertical. Then fasten a bottom cross piece at that mark (see fig. 4) with a 1" drywall screw. Attach the top cross piece in the same manner, placing it 9¾" up from the bottom of the center vertical. Then repeat to fasten another bottom cross

piece and top cross piece to another center vertical.

8. Lay out the other two verticals the same way, but position the bottom cross pieces 4⅛" and 10½" from the bottom ends of the verticals.

9. Position the first two units (see step 7) inside the long vertical assembly, opposite to each other, with the bottom of the center verticals about ¾" up from the base pieces and the cross pieces overlapping the long verticals evenly. Attach the units with 1" drywall screws at the joints.

10. Position and secure the other two units (see step 8) in the same fashion, but with their cross pieces sitting on top of the first units' cross pieces.

11. If you like, you can use a coping saw to cut angles at the ends of the

Figure 3

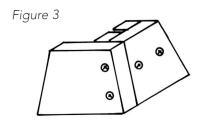

cross pieces so they'll be flush with the faces of the long verticals.

12. Using a coping saw, cut the hub into a pentagon with 1¾"-long edges. Then drill a ¼"-diameter hole through the center of the hub's face.

13. In each 1¾"-long hub edge, drill a centered ⅛"-diameter hole, ½" deep.

14. To make the rotor blades, first cut five 4½" x 13¼" rectangles from ½"-thick stock. To create the angles on the blades, use figure 5 on page 120 as a guide to mark and cut them. Sand all the edges (except the short ends) to round them.

15. In the short end of each blade, drill a centered ¼"-diameter hole, 1" deep. Then cut five 1½" lengths of ¼"-diameter dowel. Put a small dab of glue in each hole and insert a dowel. When the glue has dried, add a dab of glue to each dowel and insert the dowels into the holes in the hub, angling the blades as shown in the project photo. (One corner of each blade is aligned with a corner on the pentagonal hub.)

16. Using figure 6 on page 120 and the project photo as guides, cut the front end of the rectangular feather blank at an angle. Then glue the top edge of the feather to the bottom edge of the arrow, with the back of the feather overlapping sufficiently to cut an angle through the back of both pieces. When the glue has dried, cut the angle at the ends of these pieces.

Figure 4

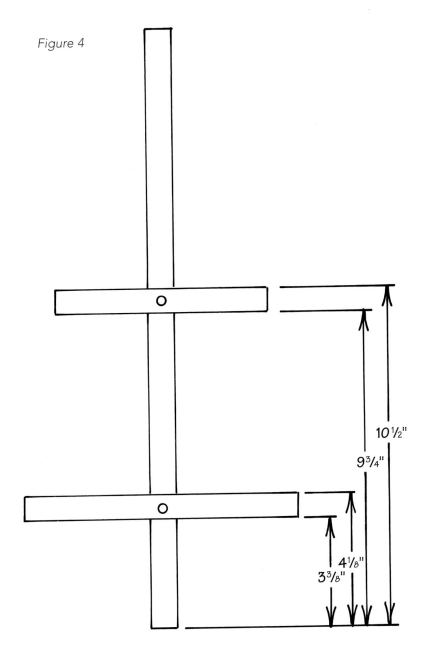

10½"

9¾"

4⅛"

3⅜"

17. Drill a centered ¼"-diameter hole though the width of the arrow, just in front of the feather, and another in the center of the arrow's front end, about 2" deep. Also drill ¼"-diameter holes through the centers of the big top and the small top.

18. Slip a ¼" flat metal washer onto a ¼" carriage bolt; then slide the bolt through the hole in the arrow. Add

another two washers to the bolt; then slip the bolt through the holes in the little top and big top. Secure the parts onto the bolt by tightening down two nuts onto the bolt's threads.

19. Place this assembly on top of the rig to see how it fits. If the threaded end of the bolt bumps up against the long verticals when you try to set the big top down onto the wide-and-narrow cap assembly, remove the arrow assembly and carefully carve away some wood from the top ends of verticals. Replace the arrow assembly on the rig. To attach the assembly, first twist the small top 45° to expose a corner of the big top's face. Insert a 1½" drywall screw through the corner of the big top and into the rig below. Twist the small top in the opposite direction to expose another corner of the big top and insert another screw. Twist the small top back into position.

20. Slip a washer onto another carriage bolt and insert the bolt through the center of the rotor hub. Add two more washers; then insert the bolt into the hole in the end of the arrow. Friction should hold the bolt in place, but you may add some glue mixed with sawdust if necessary.

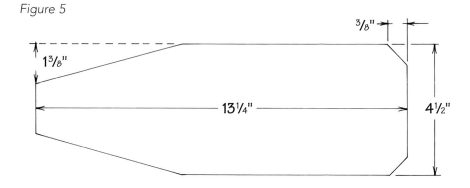

Figure 5

Figure 6

Wind Energy

imagine it—*an endless source of electricity that requires no drilling, no mining, and no pollution; one that entails no risk of toxic spills or waste, and no disputes over reserves; one for which the cost will never increase, but will actually decrease with further improvements in technology. It may sound too good to be true, but the modern wind-energy industry really does offer just such a source of electricity—not tomorrow or ten years down the road, but right now. Today.*

As you read these words, thousands of modern wind turbines are churning out clean, renewable energy all over the world. Utility-scale wind turbines provide 1.5% of the state of California's total electricity needs and more than 3% of the nation of Denmark's requirements. Smaller, non-grid-connected wind systems have brought electricity to remote villages from Alaska to India. From the enormous machines that power modern wind plants to the tiny devices that charge batteries on sailboats, wind turbines provide a safe, reliable alternative to traditional energy sources.

"But isn't wind power expensive?" you may ask. Not anymore. Many of the newest utility-scale wind plants produce electricity at a cost lower than that of nuclear energy and directly competitive with the cost of coal power. Add in the avoided cost of environmental degradation, and wind power may just be the biggest energy bargain available to utilities and their customers. And for homeowners with good wind resources, small wind turbines may offer independence from the utility grid altogether.

If you'd like to learn more about wind energy, contact one of the many local, national, and international organizations devoted to promoting this clean, renewable energy source. The European Wind Energy Association (EWEA), the American Wind Energy Association (AWEA), and the Canadian Wind Energy Association (CanWEA) all maintain excellent Internet web pages that are easily accessed with standard search engines. Soon, you'll learn all the ways that you, too, can power your home with energy from the wind.

Hummingbird *Wind Toys*

Woodworker Mike Durkin designed these busy hummingbirds, which will hover all summer—wings whirling with pleasure—wherever you want them.

Lumber and Hardware

~for one hummingbird

- 1   Pine 1 x 4, 12" long
- 1   Piece of plywood or craft wood, $\frac{1}{8}$" x 6" x 6"
- 2 $1\frac{1}{4}$" drywall screws
- 4 $\frac{1}{4}$" flat metal washers
- 2 $\frac{1}{4}$" nuts
- 1 $\frac{1}{16}$"-diameter dowel or stiff wire, 12" long

Cutting List

Number	Part Name	Dimensions
1	Body	See figure 1
2	Wing hubs	$\frac{3}{4}$" x $\frac{3}{4}$" x $\frac{3}{4}$"
2	Wings	See figure 2

Tools

Tape measure

Pencil

Jigsaw

Coping saw

Clamps

Sharp knife

Drill

$\frac{1}{16}$" and $\frac{1}{8}$" drill bits

Paintbrushes

Screwdriver

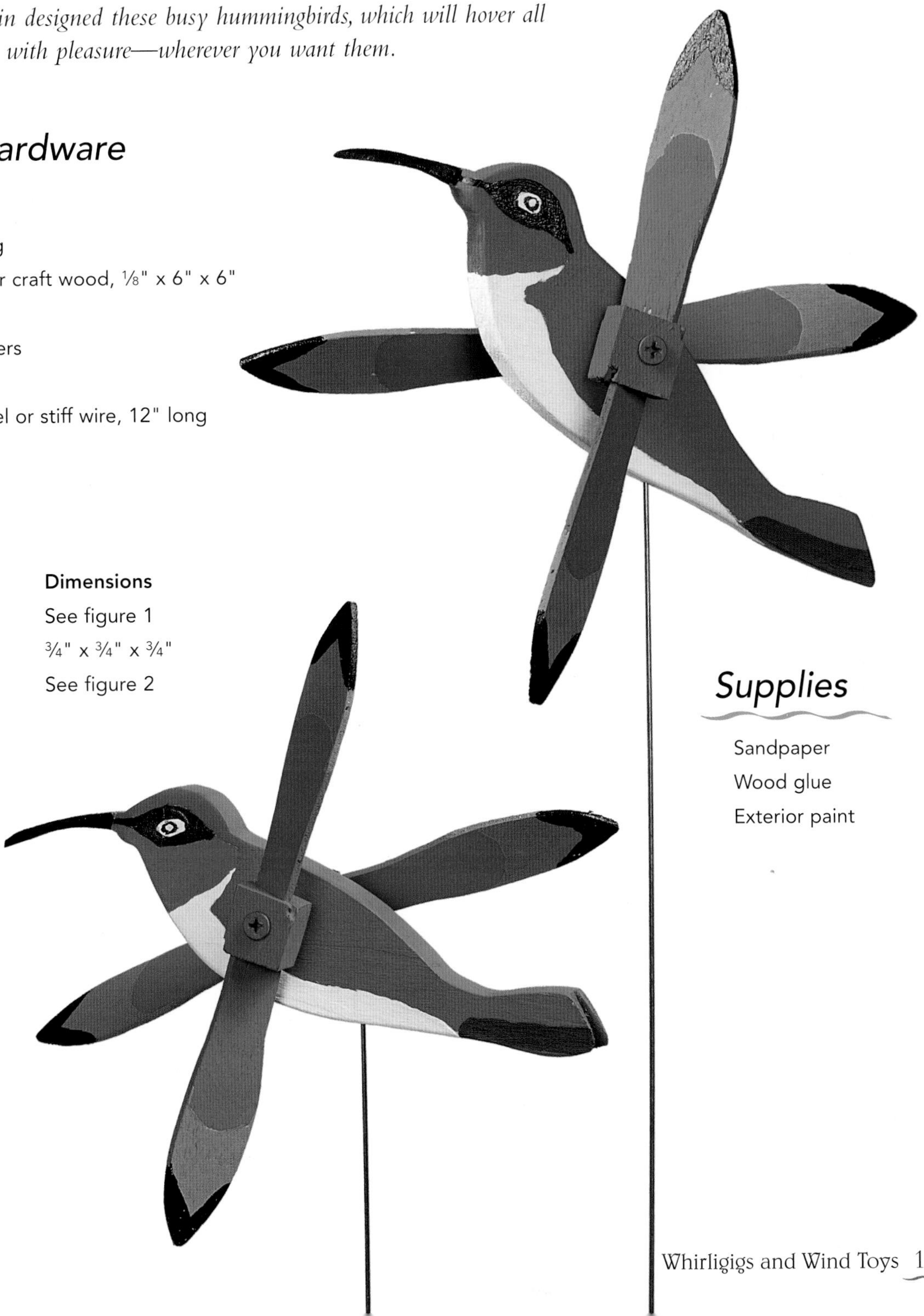

Supplies

Sandpaper

Wood glue

Exterior paint

Figure 1

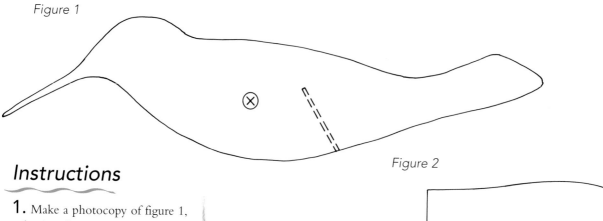

Figure 2

Instructions

1. Make a photocopy of figure 1, enlarging the pattern until the body is 7¾" long from the tip of the beak to the end of the tail. Also photocopy figure 2, enlarging the pattern until the wing is 3½" long.

2. Using the enlarged copy of figure 1, trace the outline of the body onto the pine 1 x 4. Leave some room at one end of the board for cutting the wing hubs.

3. Use a jigsaw or coping saw to cut out the body.

4. Figure 3 shows a view (from above) of the bird's beak; the inner lines represent the two cuts you must make in order to shape a ¼"-thick beak from the ¾"-thick body. First, clamp the body securely to your work surface. Then, using a coping saw, make two cuts, starting from the tip of the beak and gradually tapering each 1½"-long cut as you reach the bird's head.

5. The hummingbirds shown in the photo on page 121 have slotted tails. To make similar slots, clamp the body firmly to your work surface and cut a V-shaped section from the thickness of the tail.

6. Sand the body and beak to smooth them, supporting one side of the fragile beak with a finger or two as you sand the opposite side.

7. From the remaining piece of 1 x 4, cut two cubes to serve as wing hubs, each ¾" x ¾" x ¾".

8. To cut the wing-hub grooves into which the wings will fit, first refer to figure 4, which shows opposite sides of a wing hub. (Note that the grooves on the hub run in opposite directions.) Use a coping saw to cut the two ³⁄₁₆"-deep, ⅛"-wide diagonal grooves, carving away any excess wood with a sharp knife. Repeat to cut two grooves on the other wing hub.

9. Using a ⅛" drill bit, drill a hole through each wing hub; make sure this hole runs through the hub surfaces that don't have grooves in them.

10. Trace the enlarged wing pattern onto the plywood or craft wood. Repeat to make four wing outlines.

11. Cut out the wing shapes and sand their edges smooth.

12. Glue each wing into one of the grooves in the wing hubs (the wing ends should slide right into the grooves). Wipe away any excess glue. Make sure the glued wings are straight as the glue dries.

13. Paint the body, wing hubs, and wings, and allow the paint to dry.

14. Using a ¹⁄₁₆" drill bit, drill a pilot hole through the body piece, as shown in figure 1.

Figure 3

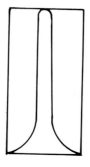

Figure 4

15. To attach each wing to the body, first slip a wing hub over a 1¼" drywall screw. Then add two ¼" flat metal washers and a ¼" nut to the screw threads. Finally, insert the tip of the screw into the pilot hole in the body, turning the screw far enough down to secure the hub and wings but leaving the assembly loose enough to allow the wings to turn freely. Repeat to attach the other hub and wings.

16. To mount the hummingbird on a length of stiff wire or on a thin dowel, drill an angled 1"-deep, ¹⁄₁₆"-diameter hole in the bottom edge of the body, as shown in figure 1. Then insert the wire or dowel in the hole, and set the hummingbirds out to spin.

Variation

This spinning bee is a variation on the Hummingbirds. The instructions are abbreviated; just refer back to the Hummingbird instructions for more details.

Tools and Materials

~for one bee

³⁄₁₆" drill bit

1 Pine 1 x 4, 10" long

1 Piece of plywood or craft wood, ⅛" x 6" x 12"

2 ³⁄₁₆"-diameter dowels, each 1½" long (see "Tips")

2 2" drywall screws

Tip

~To make the bee antennae, Mike used 1¼"-long wooden wheel axles that he found at a craft store. (The axles come with knobs on their ends.) If you have trouble finding these, use short lengths of ³⁄₁₆"-diameter dowel.

Instructions

1. Using the project photo as a guide, draw and cut a body from the 1 x 4 pine, about 4¼" long, and a head about 1⅜" long. Draw and cut from the craft wood or plywood four wings, each about 3¾" long. Sand all the pieces.

2. Bore two ³⁄₁₆"-diameter holes, ¼" deep, into the head for the antennae. Glue the antennae into the holes. Then glue the head to the body.

3. To prepare the two wing hubs read steps 7, 8, and 9 on page 122. Because the bee's wings are wider than the hummingbird's wings, you'll need to add spacers to keep them from hitting the body. Cut spacers to the same dimensions as the hubs, but don't cut grooves in them. Bore a centered ⅛" hole through each spacer.

4. Glue each wing into one of the grooves in the wing hubs and let the glue dry.

5. Bore a ⅛" pilot hole through the body piece. Then glue the spacers to the body, aligning the holes in the spacers over the pilot hole.

6. Attach each wing to the body, following step 15 above. Note that you'll be using 2" drywall screws instead of 1¼" drywall screws; you'll also omit the nuts.

7. To mount the bee, follow step 16 above.

Contributing Designers

Charlie Bennett, the talented 7-year-old who made the Lucky Horseshoe wind chime on page 46, lives in Alexander, North Carolina with his mom, dad, and three sisters.

Rachael Bennett, age 11, is always ready to try something new with fabrics. She combined her expert stitching with the fun art of marbling to make the great Swirling Colors banner featured on page 82.

Rebecca Bennett is another member of the talented Bennett family. At 8 years old, she is already a skillful designer and imaginative sewer. Rebecca created the very cheerful Happy Times flag shown on page 89 with just a little help from her older sister, Emily.

Virginia Boegli has been creating beautiful paper mache art for nearly 40 years. Her initial interest in the medium was as a tool for studying form and movement for her paintings. Today, her paper mache pieces run the gamut from delicate angels to enormous bronze replicas. Her charming Winter Birds mobile is featured on page 38. Virginia lives and works in Bozeman, Montana.

Beth Brock has been sewing for fun and function since she was a little girl. Her recent wedding to husband, David, inspired the lovely Wedding Heirloom banner on page 78. Beth and David reside in Asheville, North Carolina with their dog, Peanut.

Genevieve Burda and her husband, Larry, own and operate the Do It Best hardware store in Mars Hill, North Carolina. When she's not selling hardware or taking care of the author or the author's cat, Tucker the Amazing Demon Beast, Genevieve enjoys decorating and crafting with everyday materials. Her Gilded Leaves mobile is featured on page 47.

Robin Clark owns and operates Robin's Wood, Limited, a woodworking studio in Asheville, North Carolina. He's especially well known for his innovative bird-, bat-, and butterfly-house designs. Robin contributed the projects on pages 25, 52, 111, and 117.

Lee Davis holds an MFA degree in pottery from Indiana University. He taught at Kansas State University, Mary Baldwin College, Stuart Hall, and the Campbell Folk School before opening Birdfoot Ridge, a full-time studio located near Lee's home in Brasstown, North Carolina. Lee made the gorgeous clay wind chime on page 30.

Mike Durkin teaches woodworking to middle schoolers in Laurinburg, North Carolina where he lives with his wife, Carol. Mike is always creating something new and wonderful with wood, and his work has been featured in several books. You'll find Mike's projects on pages 28, 44, 99, 106, 121, and 123.

Margaret Gregg is an artist who loves to create new, unique designs from all varieties of fabric. She specializes in wearables, wall pieces, and sculpture. Margaret lives in Limestone, Tennessee, which is also the location of her studio. She designed the fabulous Gypsy Tiers windsock on page 61.

Jeffrey Hall stays busy running his apparel business, Diamond Gusset Jeans. When he's not navigating the vagaries of shipping blue jeans from one part of the world to another, Jeff likes to step out back to his welding shop and make gorgeous, original metal wind vanes. Some of his work is featured on pages 54, 56, and 58.

Christi Hensley lives in Barnardsville, North Carolina—right in the heart of the Blue Ridge Mountains. She owns a workshop there where she enjoys experimenting with new mediums and methods, from metal- and woodworking to paper mache. You'll find examples of Christi's latest creative forays into metal and glass work on pages 34 and 37.

Jacqueline Janes lives in Tempe, Arizona. She owns and operates the Arizona Bead Company, a mail-order business featuring a huge selection of unique and unusual beads. Thus, her choice of materials for her gorgeous Circle of Beads wind chime shown on page 41 was a natural.

Betty Kershner has been dyeing and painting silk and other fabrics for more than 20 years. Her work has been featured in numerous books, and she made the beautiful Sunset on Silk banner shown on page 87. Betty lives in Sewanee, Tennessee.

Diane Kuebitz, who lives in Sandy, Utah, draws her inspiration from whimsical spirits and natural objects. She comes from a very large and artistic family, and her son Edward is following in the family tradition by helping Diane with her ideas and designs. You'll find Diane's projects on pages 24 and 32.

Anders Lunde is one of the premier whirligig artists in the country. His work has been featured in exhibits all over the United States, and he has written several books about making whirligigs. Anders lives in Chapel Hill, North Carolina. You'll find examples of his work on pages 70 and 94.

Juanita Metcalf retired from teaching math several years ago and now works in quilting full time. She is certified by the National Quilter's Association as a teacher and judge. In addition to teaching and judging quilting, Juanita also makes gorgeous quilted items, including the lovely windsocks shown on pages 59 and 60. Juanita lives in Clyde, North Carolina.

Beth Palmer is a talented artist and decorative painter who lives in Greensboro, North Carolina. She works primarily with home accessories, but, as her Fiesta wind chime on page 42 clearly demonstrates, Beth can transform just about anything with her deft touch and inventive mind.

Carol Parks is a writer, expert sewer, and sewing consultant who lives in Asheville, North Carolina. She has written and edited several books on the subject, and you'll find her imaginative Dragonfly windsock on page 67.

Jean Wall Penland is an artist who lives in Asheville, North Carolina, where she paints and teaches. She has received both Pollock-Krasner and Adolph and Esther Gottlieb foundation grants. Jean made the fun and fanciful Jig-Time Bird flag shown on page 80.

Eric Reiswig spends his days doctoring ailing computers back to health in Victoria, British Columbia. At night, he pursues his real passion—playing traditional Irish music on uillean pipes and the penny whistle. Eric also builds wind instruments and maintains a wonderful Internet site on the subject at http://www.bc1.com/users/ereiswig. Eric made the you-have-to-hear-it-to-believe-it wind chime on page 22.

Sheila Sheppard works with contemporary materials to produce a unique range of art, from glorious wearables to fanciful objects such as the polymer clay pinwheels featured on page 113. Sheila says that she personally devises new techniques to "create images that reflect the primal spirit of ancient cultures." Sheila lives in Jonesborough, Tennessee, which is also the location of her working studio.

Don Shull describes himself as a "tinkerer." He's been tinkering with all kinds of materials for years, first as a builder and now as an artist. Recently, Don has become interested in carving, an interest he combined with his fascination with whirligigs to produce the wonderfully creepy Centipede whirligig on page 101. Don lives in Middletown, Illinois with his wife and a garden-full of unique whirligigs.

Kevin Smith worked as a mechanical engineer for years before opening the Weaverville Milling Co. Restaurant in Weaverville, North Carolina with his wife, Sally. These days, he puts that engineering knowledge to work fixing all kinds of things and creating interesting gadgets like his Shape Shifter mobile shown on page 49.

George Summers, Jr., is a multi-talented artist who works primarily in batik. He has been teaching the art of batik to children and adults for more than 20 years. George lives at Brickbottom, an artists' community in Somerville, Massachusetts. He would like to thank Lisa Horning for talking him into trying batik banners and flags, and Patty Curran for doing the sewing work on the gorgeous Oktoberfest banners featured on page 84.

Libby Woodruff is an accomplished fiber artist who works with a variety of fabrics and materials. She teaches her craft from her home studio in Big Pine, North Carolina. Libby's Butterfly windsock is featured on page 65.

Ellen Zahorec is a mixed media and studio artist living in Cincinnati, Ohio. Her work has been shown internationally and is part of numerous private and corporate collections. Ellen created the stunning Flower Garden Banners shown on pages 76 and 77.

Acknowledgments

Creating a book is never a one-person endeavor. Sincere and warm thanks go to all the people who helped bring this one together.

~ Thanks to the following folks at Lark Books (Asheville, North Carolina):

Thom Gaines, the very talented art director for this book, whose skill, impeccable taste, and hard work resulted in *Wind Toys'* wonderful, whimsical, and windy design

Chris Rich, the director of custom publishing and editor of *Wind Toys*, who held the author's hand throughout the scary, new experience of writing a book, and gave unflagging support, encouragement, and friendship

Heather Smith, the always-ready-to-help editorial assistant, who spent hours giving many of the wooden projects in this book their great-looking paint jobs.

Catharine Sutherland, the outstanding assistant editor, who, in addition to assisting with editing, also did a great deal of research and some fantastic writing, including the Vexiollogy piece on page 86.

~ Thanks also to the following great people:

Evan Bracken (Light Reflections, Hendersonville, North Carolina), whose expertise with a camera brought every project in the book to glorious life, and whose patience and good humor kept a new author from pulling out her hair

Stefan Bonitz, the very talented artist and the proprietor of Steebo's Design Studio (Asheville, North Carolina), for consultation on metalworking and for the loan of his metalworking equipment for photography

Jackie Flenner, for creating outstanding indexes, and for using her extensive knowledge of various Internet search engines to consistently locate exactly the right web sites for much of the research conducted for this book

Anders Lunde (Chapel Hill, North Carolina), for his exacting answers to endless questions about whirligigs and their construction

Eric Reiswig (Victoria, British Columbia) for sharing his exceptional knowledge of music, wind chimes, and the mysteries of Vancouver Island

Bernadette Wolf, the hard-working and efficient illustrator for *Wind Toys*, for her great illustrations and her ability to meet seemingly-impossible deadlines

~ For allowing a crew of photographers, editors, and art directors to tromp through gardens and grounds and over porches in search of the perfect shot, thanks to the following people and businesses:

Botanical Gardens at Asheville (Asheville, North Carolina); *Colby House Bed and Breakfast* (Asheville, North Carolina); *Jane Cox and Bart Murray* (Black Mountain, North Carolina); *Jim and Evelyn Grass* (Black Mountain, North Carolina); *Red Rocker Country Inn* (Black Mountain, North Carolina); *Carol and Bill Tyson* (Black Mountain, North Carolina); *Wright Inn Bed and Breakfast* (Asheville, North Carolina)

~ Thanks also to the following businesses for their assistance in the form of advice, consultation, and support:

B.B. Barnes, Inc. (Asheville, North Carolina); *Bergey Windpower* (Norman, Oklahoma)—a photo of a Bergey wind turbine appears on page 6; *Designer's Closet* (Asheville, North Carolina); *Dharma Trading Co.* (San Rafael, California); *Do It Best Hardware* (Mars Hill, North Carolina); *Earth Guild* (Asheville, North Carolina); *Enron Wind Corp.* (Tehachapi, California); *Family Dollar Store Inc.* (Asheville, North Carolina); *Foam and Fabrics Inc.* (Asheville, North Carolina); *Grovewood Gallery* (Asheville, North Carolina); *Holladay Co. Inc.* (Asheville, North Carolina); *Home Depot* (Asheville, North Carolina); *Seven Sisters Gallery* (Black Mountain, North Carolina); *Vestas American Wind Technology* (North Palm Springs, California)

Softwood Lumber Sizes

The softwood boards you buy at a lumberyard or home-improvement center—the ones you hear described as 2 x 4s or 1 x 6s—don't actually measure 2" x 4" or 1" x 6." Their actual (as opposed to "nominal") dimensions are approximately 1½" x 3½" and ¾" x 5½". Before you begin building, familiarize yourself with the differences between nominal and actual measurements. The chart that follows should prove helpful.

Softwood Lumber Sizes

Nominal	Actual
1 x 2	¾" x 1½"
1 x 4	¾" x 3½"
1 x 6	¾" x 5½"
1 x 8	¾" x 7¼"
1 x 10	¾" x 9¼"
1 x 12	¾" x 11¼"
2 x 2	1½" x 1½"
2 x 4	1½" x 3½"
2 x 6	1½" x 5½"
2 x 8	1½" x 7¼"
2 x 10	1½" x 9¼"
2 x 12	1½" x 11¼"
4 x 4	3¾" x 3½"
4 x 6	3¾" x 5½"
6 x 6	5¾" x 5½"
8 x 8	7½" x 7½"

Also note that boards of the same nominal size can vary as much as ⅛" in width or thickness. Plywood measurements, because the sheets are sanded at the mill, can also be thinner than its nominal size. Measuring lumber before you buy it will save troublesome errors during assembly.

Metric Conversion Tables

Lengths

Inches	Cm	Inches	Cm	Inches	Cm	Inches	Cm
⅛	0.3	4½	11.4	20	50.8	36	91.4
¼	0.6	5	12.7	21	53.3	37	94.0
⅜	1.0	6	15.2	22	55.9	38	96.5
½	1.3	7	17.8	23	58.4	39	99.1
⅝	1.6	8	20.3	24	61.0	40	101.6
¾	1.9	9	22.9	25	63.5	41	104.1
⅞	2.2	10	25.4	26	66.0	42	106.7
1	2.5	11	27.9	27	68.6	43	109.2
1¼	3.2	12	30.5	28	71.1	44	111.8
1½	3.8	13	33.0	29	73.7	45	114.3
1¾	4.4	14	35.6	30	76.2	46	116.8
2	5.1	15	38.1	31	78.7	47	119.4
2½	6.4	16	40.6	32	81.3	48	121.9
3	7.6	17	43.2	33	83.8	49	124.5
3½	8.9	18	45.7	34	86.4	50	127.0
4	10.2	19	48.3	35	88.9		

Volumes

1 fluid ounce	29.6 ml
1 pint	473 ml
1 quart	946 ml
1 gallon (128 fl. oz.)	3.785 l

liters x .2642 = gallons
liters x 2.11 = pints
liters x 33.8 = fluid ounces
gallons x 3.785 = liters
gallons x .1337 = cubic feet
cubic feet x 7.481 = gallons
cubic feet x 28.32 = liters

Weights

0.035 ounces	1 gram
1 ounce	28.35 grams
1 pound	453.6 grams

grams x .0353 = ounces
grams x .0022 = pounds
ounces x 28.35 = grams
pounds x 453.6 = grams
tons (short) x 907.2 = kilograms
tons (metric) x 2205 = pounds
kilograms x .0011 = tons (short)
pounds x .00045 = tons (metric)

Temperatures

To convert Fahrenheit to Centigrade (Celsius), subtract 32, multiply by 5, and divide by 9.

To convert Centigrade (Celsius) to Fahrenheit, multiply by 9, divide by 5, and add 32.

Index to Projects

Index to Subjects

continued on next page

continued from previous page